CW01429752

REVOLUTIONARY TAIWAN

REVOLUTIONARY TAIWAN

Making Nationhood in a Changing World Order

Catherine Lila Chou and Mark Harrison

Cambria Sinophone World Series
General Editor: Victor H. Mair

CAMBRIA
PRESS

Amherst, New York

Requests for permission should be directed to
permissions@cambriapress.com, or mailed to:
Cambria Press
100 Corporate Parkway, Suite 128
Amherst, New York 14226, USA.

Library of Congress Cataloging-in-Publication Data

Names: Chou, Catherine Lila, author. | Harrison, Mark, 1968- author.

Title: Revolutionary Taiwan : making nationhood in a changing world order /

Catherine Lila Chou and Mark Harrison.

Other titles: Making nationhood in a changing world order

Description: Amherst, New York : Cambria Press, [2024] |
Series: Cambria Sinophone world series |
Includes bibliographical references and index.
| Summary: "This book brings the Taiwan story to a general audience. It
will appeal to students and readers interested in international relations,
contemporary geopolitics, and East Asian Studies. Informed by years
of academic research and life in Taiwan, this book provides an entry
point to a remarkable place and people"-- Provided by publisher.

Identifiers: LCCN 2024015352 |
ISBN 9781638571957 (library binding) | ISBN 9781638573227 (paperback) |
ISBN 9781638573258 (pdf) | ISBN 9781638573265 (epub)

Subjects: LCSH: Taiwan--Foreign relations--China. | China--Foreign relations--
Taiwan. | Chinese reunification question, 1949- | Taiwan--Foreign relations--1945-
| China--Foreign relations--1949- | Taiwan--Politics and government--1945-

Classification: LCC DS799.63.C6 C47 2024 |
DDC 327.51051249--dc23/eng/20240501
LC record available at https://lccn.loc.gov/2024015352

TABLE OF CONTENTS

REVOLUTIONARY TAIWAN

PROLOGUE

This book is about the making of a Taiwanese nation, one that sees itself as a state and a homeland in its own right but has not achieved formal international recognition. Since the early 1990s, when people living in Taiwan achieved the right to freely vote for their executive and legislature, there has been a tidal change in how they view themselves and where they live. According to this view, "Taiwan" is not part of a wider, cross-strait Chinese nation, but a nation centered on the island of Taiwan itself. The outcome of democratization has been nothing less than revolutionary, producing a new, de facto nation and people that can be justly called "Taiwanese."

The imperatives of great power politics in the era of increasing US-China rivalry mean that this revolution remains unacknowledged globally. The People's Republic of China (PRC) claims sovereignty over Taiwan and insists that "reunification" is the historic mission of all peoples on both sides of the Taiwan Strait. Modern Chinese nationalism is premised in large part on the subjugation of Taiwan and its people. The PRC threatens war with and over the island, inviting a crisis that would engulf the region and beyond. Any glib judgement that the "Taiwan problem" would slip from view with "reunification" and the "rise of China" has never been less convincing.

But this Taiwan nation exists out of time. It hangs in a permanent present, the so-called "status quo," neither recognized by the international community as a fully sovereign nation nor treated by it as "part of China" the way that Chinese provinces and special administrative regions are. Yet this present could branch at any moment into radically different futures of devastating regional conflict or democratic survival and continued economic development.

Thus, Taiwan remains inaccurately recognized and poorly understood, just at the moment when Taiwanese themselves are coming into a clearer sense of their identities and accomplishments. The most common frameworks in international discourse about Taiwan—that it "split with China in 1949" or "sees itself as the true China"—fail to explain anything at all about why Taiwanese have withstood consistent pressure from the PRC to give up their democratic self-governance and their hopes for diplomatic normalization.

Each chapter of this book provides a new framework that illuminates this interstitial state and explains why democratization in Taiwan constituted a revolution, changing not just the *form* of government over the island but also how Taiwanese people conceptualized the land they lived on, as a whole and complete nation unto itself. This book also discusses the reasons why this revolution remains unfinished and contingent, as Beijing's power and the disproportionate leverage that large states exercise within the international system block off the "normal" endpoint of a revolution: an open declaration of statehood and welcome into the global community.

Chapter 1 argues that the Taiwan of today was created through not one but two struggles against Chinese party-states: the once-authoritarian Republic of China (ROC), which relocated its national government to Taiwan in 1949 after losing the Chinese Civil War, and the autocratic PRC, which has never governed the island but claims it as its territory. This first struggle transformed the ROC from a single-party dictatorship headed by the Chinese Nationalist Party (Kuomintang or KMT) into a multiparty democracy. But it did so without overthrowing the ROC or establishing a formal, globally recognized Taiwanese nation in its place. The second struggle has intensified since the 2000s. It consists not of a Cold War rivalry between "two Chinas" but the refusal by a democratic, self-consciously Taiwanese society to be annexed by the PRC, even as the Chinese Communist Party (CCP) exacts a high price for this resistance, both from Taiwanese and from the international system as a whole.

Chapter 2 presents four "alternative histories" that explain how Taiwan became a de facto independent state with a collective identity and way of life that differs significantly from that of modern China. The first is Taiwan's 6,000-year history as an indigenous homeland, a land that has been repeatedly colonized and has yet to be fully decolonized. The second, Taiwan's century-long history of struggle for self-determination, beginning with movements for self-rule during the Japanese era in the early twentieth century. The third, Taiwan's mid-century unification with China (the ROC), an experience of military occupation and martial law that offers a glimpse of what unification with China (the PRC) might be like. And the fourth, Taiwan as a place that is often denied both a history and future because of the directive that it is "supposed to be" or "will be" part of China.

Chapter 3 uses the KMT's renaming of the streets of Taipei after places in China in the 1950s as a starting point to argue that the ROC was a colonial power in Taiwan. It then explores how this colonial image of Taiwan has been wielded against present-day Taiwanese as evidence that they are naturally and essentially Chinese. Today, Taiwan is rarely called "Taiwan" in international organizations and events but must be referred to with other labels, "Chinese Taipei" among them, to accede to the PRC's nationalist ideology. Both as a map that can be traced through the streets of post-war Taipei, and as a name intended to hide, humiliate, and hinder Taiwan, "Chinese Taipei" helps to explain the tragedies of Taiwan's modern history and the way that it has been misnamed and marginalized to serve the ideologies of two successive Chinese party-states.

Chapter 4 argues that Taiwan's existence expresses the contradictions of the post–World War II international system itself, which holds out the promise of self-determination and sovereignty for peoples under international law while also allowing economically and militarily powerful states to disproportionately shape the system in their interests. Both excluded from the global community and at the heart of the world's anxieties over war and nuclear destruction, Taiwan is treated less a real place than a haunting presence that makes the contradictions of the international system visible. It becomes an "issue" or a "problem" in which the prospects for peace or war in the world are simultaneously visible. The result is that national and local governments, NGOs, and individual people help to erase Taiwan and Taiwanese people either at the behest of Chinese government officials or preemptively in response to often undefined calculations about the prospect of war over the island.

Finally, the epilogue explores what it means to flourish in the face of an existential threat, while also dealing with the limitations of a nationhood that is unrecognized by global institutions and national governments, and in a multitude of minor ways on various websites, academic publications, and global media reports. The "China problem" is the critical question that structures modern Taiwanese life. China regularly threatens war and has carried out a military buildup across the Strait unprecedented in peacetime. These threats are intended to keep Taiwanese people in line, guessing about what China's true red lines are. The "China problem" steals time, money, and many other resources not only from quality-of-life issues in Taiwan but also from the long-term planning and policy changes necessary to ensure that there will be a healthy Taiwanese society, state, and economy decades into the future.

This book places Taiwan at its center. This is a necessarily and unavoidably a political act. From the vantage point of empires and powerful states, Taiwan is a symbol of their visions for greatness, and the limitations of these ambitions. In the late seventeenth century, the Qing dynasty treated Taiwan as a troublesome maritime flank of an empire more interested in west and central Asia. For Imperial Japan in the early twentieth century, Taiwan was supposed to be a model colony, the first of many in its disastrous plan for modern industrialized imperialism in East and Southeast Asia. During the Cold War at mid-century, the US called Taiwan "Free China" to contrast it with Communist China and demonstrate the superiority of the American-led international order, although Taiwan under one-party KMT rule was not free at all. Today, Beijing says Taiwan's unification with the PRC will complete the "Great Rejuvenation of the Chinese nation," even though this goal arguably moves further out of reach every year.

Being Taiwanese, as this book shows, is an exercise in being subject to such historical and geopolitical forces, which together create multiple overlapping realities. Taiwanese people today inhabit a territory variously described as "Taiwan," "the ROC," "the ROC (Taiwan)," "Chinese Taipei," "Taiwan, Province of China" or often just as "part of China," and they are targeted by more foreign disinformation than any other people in the world.[1] Yet Taiwanese aspirations for nation building and democracy have grown ever more urgent since the early twentieth century, thus far thwarting Taiwan's absorption into yet another would-be empire. Taiwanese have expressed their resistance to power through dissent and sometimes violence from the late Qing era right through Japanese colonialism, KMT authoritarianism, and the threat of invasion by the PRC. The belief that there is an authentic Taiwan that has yet to be properly recognized by both Taiwanese and the world at large has endured and matured through rule by successive colonial regimes.

We argue that while Taiwan's nationhood remains a radical position from the perspective of the post–World War II international system, this nationhood is normal to Taiwanese people and already broadly accepted by them. To illustrate this, we situate this book in the everyday in Taiwan, narrating instances from electoral, social, cultural, environmental, and urban life that showcase how Taiwanese people experience their homeland. If this book is political, it is a politics of the normal, describing the hope by the Taiwanese of a normal national life free of threats and unencumbered by its existence as a geopolitical flashpoint. In Taiwan's overlapping and doubled realities, the normal is radical.

A radical politics of the normal also informs our hope to provide a readable account of such a complex story. There is a surfeit of recent good journalism about Taiwan. There is also a growing number of scholarly monographs in the field of Taiwan studies. This book fills a need for an accessible entry point and general introduction to Taiwan. It guides the reader through an encounter with Taiwan that goes beyond a linear historical overview or a neatly divided chapter-by-chapter exploration of Taiwanese politics, society, economics, and security. The need for such a book is itself a sign of Taiwan's spectral international presence coming into clearer focus. For in this emerging era, the people of Taiwan have made themselves heard as never before.

NOTES

1. V-Dem Annual Report Team, "Democracy Facing Global Challenges", p. 34.

CHAPTER 1

TWO CHINAS AGAINST
A TAIWANESE NATION

COUNTING THE TRUTH

Elections in Taiwan are distinctively public. After the polls close on election Saturdays, everyone—including journalists, party staff, community members, children, citizens and non-citizens alike—is free to visit their neighborhood polling place to watch the votes being counted. In the count, one teller holds up paper ballots to the assembled audience and calls the vote out loud and another teller repeats it. This ritual is called *changpiao* 唱票, literally "to sing the vote." The votes are recorded in groups of five on long strips of paper, forming column after column of the five-stroke Chinese character *zheng* 正, meaning "just" or "correct." Anyone present is empowered to point out errors in the tallying.

Vote counting in Taiwan is not merely a bureaucratic process. Every single one of the votes—more than fourteen million votes cast for president and vice president in January 2020—is called out loud.[1] This "old-fashioned" counting process is designed to counter ballot rigging, a once common practice in local elections prior to full democracy, and to instill confidence in the results. On election nights, *changpiao* can take on the emotional force of liturgy. To witness vote counting is to feel viscerally how much democracy has transformed every aspect of life here in the thirty years since the end of authoritarian rule. The process is also open, clean, and surprisingly fast. The president is elected in a first past-the-post count, while 107 legislative seats are determined by geographic constituencies and party lists generated by registered political parties. There are also six legislative seats reserved for indigenous Taiwanese. Victory and concession speeches take place before the evening is out.

In contrast to the seriousness of vote counting, Taiwanese election campaigns are very noisy and emotional, dominating public life on television and on the streets for months. Furious combative political talk shows like "Taiwan: Go for It!" (*Tâi-oân hiòng-chiân kiâⁿ* 台灣向前行!) and "News Straight Talk" (*xinwen dabaihua* 新聞大白話) feature hours of running commentary every night. Clips of press conferences and photo opportunities are overlaid with hosts and guests heaping praise or opprobrium upon politicians in a cacophonous, argumentative style. For months beforehand, campaign trucks with flags and megaphones drive around Taiwan's cities and towns blasting music and campaign slogans, while the streetscapes are taken over by colorful flags and billboards.

As in other democratic polities, elections in Taiwan offer a glimpse into the minds of the voters at a particular moment in time. Housing prices, pensions, taxes, healthcare, urban development are all issues that sway votes. Taiwanese elections, however, also perform a unique function that give them both global and local consequences: they challenge the view that Taiwan is a "province of China" and subject to Beijing's rule in the same way that Guangdong or Fujian, or any of the other provinces of the People's Republic of China (PRC, Zhonghua renmin gongheguo 中華人民共和國) are. Although Taiwan is routinely described as a "wayward" or "renegade" province in English-language media, the Chinese Communist Party (CCP, Zhongguo gongchandang 中國共產黨) has never controlled it.[2] In China, no provincial executives or legislators are elected by plebiscite, and no officials from the PRC have ever exerted any jurisdiction over Taiwan. This makes Taiwan substantively different from Hong Kong, Xinjiang, and Tibet, three borderland territories that are governed as part of the PRC and whose people Beijing is disciplining according to standards of linguistic, ethnic, and ideological purity expected of loyal "mainland citizens."

The CCP, which has governed the PRC since its inception in 1949, proclaims Taiwan as both its present and future territory. But Taiwanese direct elections—for the legislature since 1992, and the president since 1996—are continuing proof of the island's de facto independence. They are just one of many empirical challenges to the narrative about a "unified China" that Beijing imposes both within its own borders and, increasingly, on other governments and their citizens as well.

Given this, it is not surprising that the major cleavage in Taiwanese politics is about China and how to manage a relationship that is both economically interdependent and politically and militarily threatening. Two major political parties and camps have developed around this "China cleavage."[3] The Chinese Nationalist Party (Zhongguo Guomindang 中國 國民黨), also known by its Mandarin transliteration Kuomintang (KMT), took control of Taiwan from Japan in 1945, fled to the island after losing the Chinese Civil War in 1949, and governed Taiwan as a one-party state for nearly forty-five years after that. It holds that Taiwan and China are two parts of a state that has yet to be knit back together, while leaving unanswered the crucial question of what name or political system this prospective "one China" should adopt. The Democratic Progressive Party (DPP, Minzhu jinbudang 民主進步黨), founded in September 1986 just before the KMT lifted martial law, rejects the idea that Taiwan is part of a cross-Strait Chinese nation. With an eye on Taiwan's security, however, it continues to defer the question of whether to declare a new Taiwanese republic. Since 2014, several third parties have emerged, most notably the Taiwan People's Party (TPP, Taiwan minzhongdang 台灣民 眾黨), which promised to chart a pathway between the KMT and DPP on the "China cleavage" and secured five legislative seats in the 2020 elections, a number that increased to eight in 2024. (As of the publication of this book in 2024, however, TPP legislators faced accusations of KMT partisanship after allying with the party to form narrow majorities in the newest legislature.)[4]

The PRC does not respect the principle of democratic elections in Taiwan if they produce an outcome incongruent with its irredentist ideologies. In January 2016, Tsai Ing-wen 蔡英文 of the DPP, a legal academic, former trade negotiator, and celebrated owner of two cats, Think Think 想想 and Ah-Tsai 阿蔡, won the presidency against the KMT candidate Eric Chu 朱立倫. Her party also secured a legislative majority, the first time a non-KMT party gained control of both branches of government. The PRC responded to her election with a campaign of intimidation intended to make her a one-term president by stepping up efforts to influence Taiwan's information environment, including setting up content farms, purchasing social media accounts, creating fake news, and magnifying the homegrown skepticism of some Taiwanese about the qualifications of DPP members to govern.[5] The PRC cut off official contact with Taipei and moved to further constrict Taiwan's already limited international space. It leaned on the World Health Organization (WHO) to refrain from inviting Taiwan to their annual assembly as an observer. In July 2019, the Chinese Ministry of Tourism and Culture stopped issuing individual travel permits to Taiwan.[6] Between 2017 and 2019, Beijing established relations with six countries—Panama, Burkina Faso, the Dominican Republic, El Salvador, Kiribati, and Solomon Islands —on the precondition that they drop official ties and end all aid and investment programs with the government in Taipei.[7] In the last instance, Taiwanese officials literally knocked on the apartment doors of Solomon Island students in Taipei to inform them they had to leave the following day. *Bloomberg* reported that "With the Solomon Islands' break, China has reduced Taiwan's formal diplomatic footprint by 46% in terms of population and 52% in terms of economic output since Tsai came to power."[8]

Just how far from or close to China, just how safe or imperiled Taiwan might be, because of a DPP or KMT (or perhaps TPP) administration taking the helm in any election remains unpredictable. The exact threat that China poses, and the possibility and timeline of a military incursion, are unknowable just from observing its opaque policymaking. In the meantime, the "China cleavage" steals time and resources from domestic quality-of-life and human rights issues in Taiwan, such as gender equality, immigration, labor conditions, low salaries, energy production, and environmental protection.

As a result, electioneering in Taiwan can induce feelings of deja vu. Instead of interrogating government policy proposals and legislative programs, the same questions are asked again and again by domestic, and especially foreign, observers about China. Does this election bring the Taiwanese people closer to accepting "reunification" under the "one country, two systems" arrangement applied to Hong Kong, or closer to "independence," which could mean military conflict? For decades, a great deal of international commentary on the status of Taiwan has begun with the assumption that cool heads and sober analysis regard unification, and Taiwan's disappearance as a unique place of its own, as inevitable and desirable. Perhaps, if the PRC improved its human rights record, Taiwanese might suddenly find the prospect of political union with China appealing. Or, if China becomes powerful enough, the people of Taiwan will simply accept unification and their own erasure as their only option. Taiwan is sometimes characterized as a "Chinese democracy," a framing that is meant to counter Orientalist stereotypes about the suitability of people with "Chinese" ancestry to self-governance.[9] As members of a "Chinese democracy," Taiwanese stand in for their counterparts on "the mainland," pointing the way towards a future for optimistic Western pundits in which all Chinese people will live under a liberal democratic and unified regime.

These questions are generated not by any organic desire for "unification" from the Taiwanese electorate but rather by geopolitical forces that are seeking a specific set of answers about great power competition and the future of the international order. In ten years of surveys by Taiwan's Mainland Affairs Council (MAC, Dalu weiyuanhui 大陸委員會), the highest recorded percentage of Taiwanese to support "unification as soon as possible" was 4.5% (in August 2018). The option of "maintaining the status quo [now] and unification later" scored a recorded high of 16% (in October 2018).[10] Even many of those who vote and describe themselves as KMT, therefore, have expressed little desire to be incorporated into the PRC or another iteration of "one China." Support for the KMT today often derives more from identity politics (for instance, appealing to the nostalgia of older generations whose families escaped China in the mid-twentieth century), as well as a pragmatic view that it is less confrontational towards China than the DPP, than from the desire to rule or live in a cross-Strait Chinese nation.

Elections in Taiwan are thus a paradox: each contest at the ballot box is not solely about China, and yet electoral results in their totality impact relations with China. Elections thus take on an upside-down meaning. They reduce not to the everyday concerns of ordinary voters, in accordance with the aphorism that all politics is local, but instead gesture upwards to the forces of geopolitics. The outcome of every major campaign is read for what it says about Taiwan's position towards China and what this might mean for the direction of strategic competition between China and the United States both regionally and globally.

On the night of January 11, 2020, Tsai Ing-wen was reelected as president by the people of Taiwan. She received 8.1 million votes to the 5.5 million cast for her KMT challenger, Han Kuo-yu 韓國瑜, a remarkable turnaround from predictions a year prior. By election day, DPP officials had been more confident that Tsai herself would win, but their optimism was tempered by the party's prospects for the legislature. Losing their majority would allow the KMT to stall Tsai's second term legislative agenda. Against these predictions, the DPP comfortably retained its legislative majority at the conclusion of the *changpiao*.

With this announcement, crowds squeezed shoulder-to-shoulder into the streets in front of DPP headquarters on Beiping East Road in the Zhongzheng District of Taipei to celebrate. Stalls sold Tsai Ing-wen themed piggy banks and keychains, as well as hot sweet sausages and glutinous rice on sticks. Supporters waved yellow and pink banners emblazoned with Tsai's campaign slogan, "Let's Win" (*Taiwan yaoying* 台灣要贏), a play on the Mandarin pronunciation of the second character of her name, *ing* 英. The slogan thus literally meant "Taiwan must win" but could also be read as "Taiwan wants Tsai Ing-wen."

While the result was a comprehensive win for Tsai and the DPP, a feeling of contingency—of a stable and secure future always deferred—ran like an undercurrent through her victory rally. Some attendees carried green and cerulean flags advocating for a formal Taiwanese nation, a reminder of aspirations that even an administration that sees itself as proudly Taiwanese cannot fulfill. "I stand for Taiwanese independence" (*Taiwan duli* 台灣獨立) and "Let's build a Taiwanese nation" (*Taiwan ren jian Taiwanguo* 台灣人建台灣國), they proclaimed. On these flags, Taiwan was represented not as an island off the coast of China but as a whale swimming freely in the Pacific Ocean or as a Formosan black bear, an endemic species that has a distinctive white V-shaped marking on its chest. Standing out in the colorful sea of Tsai- and Taiwan-related imagery were large black flags emblazoned with "Liberate Hong Kong, Revolution of Our Times" (*guangfu xianggang, shidaigeming* 光復香港，時代革命) in English and Cantonese. They were carried by Hong Kongers displaced after the massive summer 2019 protests against an extradition bill that would allow criminal suspects to be transferred across the border to face mainland justice.[11]

Once the vote was formally confirmed by the Central Election Commission, President Tsai arrived on the stage to give her acceptance speech. She began by saying, "I would like to thank everyone who voted today. Regardless of how you voted, by taking part in this election you have put democratic values into practice. With each presidential election, Taiwan is showing the world how much we cherish our free, democratic way of life, and how much we cherish our nation: the Republic of China, Taiwan...”[12]

TAIWAN, THE REPUBLIC OF CHINA, AND THE REPUBLIC OF CHINA (TAIWAN)

In the official transcript of Tsai's speech, the name of this "nation" is written as "the Republic of China (Taiwan)," with an awkward paren-thetical. For while these elections took place on the island of Taiwan —and the smaller outlying islands of Kinmen, Matsu, Penghu, Green Island, and Orchid Island—they were held for positions in a state called the Republic of China (ROC), which has governed these island territories since 1945, following the redrawing of national and imperial borders by the Allied victory in World War II.

This chapter argues that it is not only the People's Republic but also this other, simultaneously existing (Republic of) China that has stood against the recognition of a nation-state known as "Taiwan." In the pages that follow, we lay out the relationship of the ROC to Taiwan and the reasons why the two have merged in recent years, the former both constricting and in some ways protecting the latter. The ROC is often described as Taiwan's "official name," a shorthand that obscures just how, when, and why, the histories of two places came to intersect, and what it might mean for them to diverge. No one living in Taiwan at mid-century had a choice to accept or reject becoming part of the ROC. Today, it is the ROC government that is still recognized by 12 out of the 193 United Nations (UN) member states, plus the Holy See. The Central Bank of the ROC that mints the local currency (New Taiwan Dollars), the ROC Ministry of Foreign Affairs that issues passports for travel and identification, and the ROC army that is tasked with defending Taiwan in the event of war. As a result of democratization, and the right of Taiwanese people to express their identities and political opinions that it brought, the ROC has become a hybrid state identity, with "Taiwan" sometimes appended to it after a comma or in a parenthetical; or used in place of "the ROC" entirely, especially in informal settings. Through this historical process, Taiwanese people have come to live simultaneously in overlapping spaces and realities: Taiwan, the Republic of China (ROC), ROC Taiwan, and ROC (Taiwan). Today, it is not ROC authoritarianism imposing an ROC identity onto Taiwan but a new force—the rise of the People's Republic of China—that prevents the people of Taiwan from choosing to shed the ROC identity altogether or to declare a new Taiwanese nation.

Yet Taiwan's history far predates that of the ROC (and the PRC). The island has been home to dozens of Austronesian-language First Nations for some six thousand years, each with their own languages, cultural traditions, and relationships to Taiwan's diverse ecologies and topographies. Not until the early seventeenth century was Taiwan pulled into the era of empire, when parts of the north, around present-day Keelung, were claimed as a crown colony under Spain's King Philip IV, and parts of the southwest, centered on the modern city of Tainan, were claimed by the Dutch East India Company, the Verenigde Oostindische Compagnie (VOC). The first significant waves of settlers from China to make their homes year-round in Taiwan came at the encouragement of the Dutch to farm the land and secure camphor and deer pelts for colonial profit.[13]

Since the brief era of European colonization of the island, political upheaval and revolution in early modern and modern China have been major forces shaping Taiwan's history and demographics. In 1662, as the Ming dynasty was falling to the Qing in China, Taiwan became an outpost for a Ming loyalist pirate known as Koxinga or Zheng Chenggong 鄭成功, who expelled the Dutch and established the short-lived Kingdom of Tungning (Dongning wangguo 東寧王國). When Koxinga's descendants were in turn defeated by the Qing in 1683, the island of Taiwan was gradually incorporated into a cross-Strait Chinese empire for the first time. In the two hundred years of Qing rule over the western part of Taiwan, colonists from China came to greatly outnumber indigenous peoples in the north, west, and south, exerting increasing pressure on their land, livelihoods, and sovereignty via land expropriation and intermarriage. These settlers pushed eastward from the coastal plains, sometimes with the sanction of distant Qing officials but very often against imperial policy.[14] In 1885, as the Qing empire was beset by internal strife and external encroachment, the government bestowed provincial status upon Taiwan, in response to a failed French invasion. Then, in 1895, as the Qing dynasty entered its twilight years, Taiwan was ceded to Japan "in perpetuity" under the Treaty of Shimonoseki, as part of the settlement of the First Sino-Japanese War of 1894–1895.

Taiwan remained a Japanese colony for fifty years. The Japanese Empire was the first to claim and administer the entirety of the island, through its brutal, methodical suppression of uprisings and rebellions as well as its massive investment in infrastructure and resource extraction.[15] Historian Evan Dawley argues that a distinct Taiwanese identity first began to develop in this period, as Chinese migrants and descendants, abandoned by the Qing, were alternately subject to assimilationist and exclusionist policies and came to define themselves as ethnically and culturally Taiwanese in contrast to their new colonizers and to the island's indigenous populations. In the 1920s and 1930s, a large-scale movement began petitioning the imperial Diet in Tokyo for self-government for Taiwan against the furious opposition of Taiwan's colonial administration.[16]

In China, meanwhile, the Xinhai Revolution against the Qing dynasty led to the founding of the Republic of China (ROC) on January 1, 1912, under the leadership of the KMT and party founder and provisional president, Dr. Sun Yat-sen 孫逸仙. By this time Taiwan had already been a Japanese colonial territory for sixteen years, and the first provisional constitution of the ROC declared that the "territory of the Chinese republic consists of twenty-two provinces"—the provinces that were part of the Qing Empire at its demise—plus "Inner and Outer Mongolia, Tibet, and Qinghai," but not Taiwan.[17] The ROC constitutions of 1923 and 1931 also did not claim Taiwan as Chinese territory.[18] For a decade between 1927 and

1937, China was a one-party state under KMT governance, although the effectiveness of central rule varied considerably across different regions of the country as warlords fought for power and maintained contingent levels of commitment to the new Republic. The CCP was founded in 1921 as a challenger to the KMT and, with the brutal crackdown on Communists in Shanghai starting in April 1927, the two parties began a violent struggle that developed into a civil war that continued until 1949. When the Japanese Imperial Army invaded China in 1937, Taiwan had already been part of the Japanese Empire for more than four decades. As Maria Adele Carrai notes in her study of the concept of sovereignty in modern Chinese history, it was only in the 1930s that maps of the ROC began to include territories, such as Taiwan, that had once been governed by previous Chinese dynasties.[19]

The trajectories of Taiwan and the Republic of China (ROC) intersected at the end of World War II, when Imperial Japan was stripped of its colonial possessions and the KMT occupied the island by agreement of the victorious Allies. Although this arrangement was billed as a "retrocession" or "restoration" (*guangfu* 光復), Taiwan had never before been part of the ROC, nor were the six million people already living there offered a say by the great powers in their postwar fate. They did not, for example, choose the 1947 ROC constitution, which now added Taiwan to its existing twenty-two provinces. The overlap in distant heritage between the KMT and most of the inhabitants of the island hid the re-colonization of Taiwan behind a rhetoric of return to a correct territorial order.

Conflict between people in Taiwan and the new administration arose almost immediately over corruption, bribery, inflation, and the seizure of capital and industry, exacerbated by KMT distrust of a population whose collective experience of the Japanese Empire in the 1930s and 1940s had differed so much from their own. In early 1947, a seemingly minor confrontation incited a defining period of political violence, known as the February 28th Incident. Customs officials operating outside of

Tianma Tea House in Taipei attempted to confiscate contraband from a cigarette seller, a widow named Lin Chiang-mai 林江邁. Outraged witnesses gathered, and a panicked officer fired into the crowd. This local disturbance soon escalated to uprisings across the island against the KMT administration, which called in reinforcements from across the Strait and quelled the protests with extreme violence. Estimates range from ten to twenty thousand people killed. Far from being accepted as natural or normal, the process of "reunification" with the (Republic of) China was contested at a terrible cost.[20]

Since the February 28th uprisings, the Republic of China has coexisted in conflict with the desire of many Taiwanese to establish a new independent nation called Taiwan. Two incommensurable realities, narratives, and future aspirations have thus been mapped onto the island.

Although the ROC began its existence outside of Taiwan, it soon became utterly dependent on the island and its existing population for survival when the KMT was defeated by the CCP in the Chinese Civil War in 1949. With the founding of the PRC, the KMT leadership, military and nearly three-quarters of a million refugees fled to the island. This latest wave of mass migration from China came to account for about fifteen percent of the total population of modern Taiwan, ranging from Republican elites and military officials to rank-and-file KMT soldiers, civilian supporters, children, and poor and working-class individuals who had been coerced into joining the military or serving the party.[21] The exiled regime was by turns aspirational, delusional, and paranoid in its behavior. Taiwan became a staging ground for the KMT's hope to "retake the mainland" (*fangong dalu* 反攻大陸) by force, a site on which the party leadership played out the fiction that it was still the legitimate ruler of China. Taiwan also became figured as an idealized China in miniature, one whose achievements would allegedly inspire the Chinese on the mainland to throw off the yoke of Communism. In the civil service, ninety-five percent of positions were reserved for Nationalist refugees, on the principle that Taiwan was only one province out of twenty-three in the ROC.[22] Similarly, seats in the Legislative Yuan (Lifayuan 立法院) and the (now-defunct) National Assembly (Guomin dahui 國民大會) were held by representatives of mainland provinces who had been elected in the 1947–1948 elections. They held their seats until death, replaced by the runners-up (if they were still alive); this practice continued right up to the early 1990s.

The new logic of the Cold War meant that the KMT's implausible quest was soon supported by the United States. After 1947, the US had equivocated on propping up the KMT against the CCP and effectively abandoned them by the beginning of 1950. However, with the outbreak of the Korean War on June 25, 1950, President Harry Truman reversed the US position and ordered the Seventh Fleet into the Taiwan Strait to provide both precautionary military protection to the ROC and to tacitly constrain any rash attempt by the Nationalists to launch a renewed offensive against the new People's Republic. Formal US support lasted until 1979, when the US ended its military presence in Taiwan and withdrew its diplomatic recognition of the ROC government.

In the moral geography of Cold War–era America, Taiwan was the righteous "Free China" standing against "Red China." But "Free China" was a fiction, as Taiwan itself descended into a prolonged period of violent authoritarianism known as the White Terror. The project of transforming Taiwan into the fictional ROC and maintaining the illusion that it was the real China was carried out through the discipline and punishment of the people who lived on the island and a handful of smaller outlying ones still controlled by the ROC military, such as the Pescadores (Penghu), as well as Kinmen (Quemoy) and Matsu, just kilometers away from the mainland. During the period of martial law (1949–1987), the government claimed it was readying to defeat the Communists in Beijing, recited in hollow slogans like "Fight Communism and Recover China" (*fangong fuguo* 反共復國) that dominated Taiwan's public life. However, most of the coercive functions of the military and security services, called the Garrison Command (Jingbei zongsilingbu 警備總司令部), were directed domestically towards the repression of suspected dissidents. Victims included both those who called the island home before 1945 and the less fortunate of the refugees who arrived with the KMT in 1949. An estimated 140,000 people were sentenced for political crimes that included reading banned material, joining underground Communist groups, and supporting Taiwanese nationalism, sometimes to prison terms of a decade or more. At least 1,000 were sentenced to death and killed by the state.[23]

The "ROC on Taiwan" occluded Taiwan itself for much of the second half of the twentieth century. In the 1970s, these infolded realities began to shift as geopolitics brought the US and the PRC closer, and the ROC came to be seen as increasingly illegitimate. The ROC had held the China seat in the United Nations, including in the Security Council, since 1945, but as PRC influence grew, the exclusion of over eight hundred million people in China from UN representation became untenable. The KMT dictator Chiang Kai-shek 蔣介石, who was born in Zhejiang Province in 1887 and had never visited Taiwan before escaping there in 1949, rejected opportunities for dual recognition or for a "One China, One Taiwan" solution.[24] So too did his PRC counterparts. In 1971, the UN General Assembly passed Resolution 2758, expelling "the representatives of Chiang Kai-shek" and finally handing the seat reserved for "China" from the ROC to the PRC. Although the resolution did not mention Taiwan, it effectively left all residents of Taiwan without access to this key multilateral organization. Both Taiwan and the Republic of China now stood largely outside the postwar international system. Although the ROC was losing the recognition of many of the world's nation-states in the 1970s, neither the KMT nor the CCP would permit a formal Taiwanese state to emerge in its place.

Still, Taiwan began to take shape in this decade as a polity that governments were sometimes willing to engage with informally. In 1979, the United States also recognized the PRC as the sole legitimate government of China, abrogating the Sino-American Mutual Defense Treaty signed in 1954 with the ROC. In its place, Congress passed the

Taiwan Relations Act, authorizing the creation of a de facto but unofficial embassy in Taipei, known as the American Institute in Taiwan (AIT), and setting forth a framework for arms sales to the "governing authorities on Taiwan." Since then, the United States has remained committed to a tactic of strategic ambiguity on Taiwan's defense, leaving open the question of how or if the US would respond to a military crisis in the Taiwan Strait. The US "one China" policy (taking no official position on the status of Taiwan) has created room for different presidential administrations and Congresses to craft policies that offered varying levels of military, moral, and geopolitical support to Taiwan over the years.[25]

Just as it was facing a shrinking diplomatic footprint abroad, the KMT government was also contending with a hard-fought movement for democracy within Taiwan marked by demonstrations, occupations, hunger strikes, guerilla broadcasts, strategic arrests, defiance of speech and publishing controls, and illicit fundraising from abroad, designed to galvanize the broader public and capture the attention of international press and human rights groups. At the core of this movement, known as the *dangwai* 黨外 (for "outside the party," that is, outside the KMT), was the articulation of a Taiwanese identity and a demand for people who called themselves such to determine a democratic future of their homeland. The *dangwai* was dominated by Taiwanese-language speakers, known as Hoklo Taiwanese, the majority ethnolinguistic group on the island, but it also included Hakka Taiwanese, indigenous Taiwanese, and dissident "mainlanders." The anti-authoritarian activism of this period was eclectic in nature. Some activists limited their agenda to reforming the ROC system, to allow for free elections and give native-born Taiwanese a proportionate share of power. Others called for the overthrow of the KMT and ROC and the creation of a new Taiwanese nation. On September 28, 1986, in a key turning point, *dangwai* leaders gathered at the Grand Hotel overlooking Taipei, built by the Chiang regime to welcome the had steadily diminishing numbers of visiting foreign dignitaries. In a dramatic move, the meeting attendees paraded a new party flag through the hotel meeting room and declared the founding of the Democratic Progressive Party. It was, at that moment, an illegal act. But a new Taiwan was emerging and the arrests that the activists expected never came. Concessions by Chiang Ching-kuo 蔣經國 (Chiang Kai-shek's son) in the months just before his death on January 13, 1988, helped ensure that the DPP and its supporters achieved major goals: the end of martial law and the implicit legalization of opposition parties.[26]

The change in the social and political mood was rapid. After decades spent claiming that it was a sacred mission to "recover the mainland" by force, the KMT quietly abandoned this goal at its thirteenth party congress in 1988, under the leadership of the new president Lee Teng-hui 李登輝, the first Taiwan-born leader of the ROC.[27] Lee was an agricultural economist and technocrat born in colonial Taiwan and educated in Japan who had improbably risen through the ranks of the KMT to succeed Chiang Ching-kuo. In March 1990, a six-day mass student protest known as the Wild Lily Movement (Yebaihe xueyun 野百合學運) called for direct elections of the president, vice president, and legislative members. Lee acceded to their demands and established a constitutional convention to reform the system of government. The outcome was the promulgation of the first Additional Articles of the Constitution (Xianfa Zengxiu Tiaowen 憲法增修條文) in 1991–1992, which limited the rights of full political participation, now including direct elections of the executive and legislature, to qualified voters residing in the "Free Area of the ROC" (Ziyou diqu 自由地區), as opposed to the "Chinese mainland area." This legal distinction between Taiwan and the mainland acknowledged that the ROC now only controlled Taiwan and its outlying islands. For more than three decades, the Additional Articles have served as the fundamental law of the ROC, designed to "meet the requisites of the nation" "prior to national unification." The architects of this change tacitly accepted that unification could no longer be pursued without public approval, which is nearly nonexistent today.[28]

Writing a new constitution altogether would likely be regarded by the PRC as a formal declaration of Taiwanese independence and a potential trigger for military action. The constitutional reforms that enabled Taiwan's modern democracy still must accommodate an imaginary ROC that covers all of China, for fear of disastrous conflict. Thus, they reflect Taiwan's circumstance as a nation suspended in time between a lost ROC past and an unrealized future of international normalization and recognition.[29]

During his twelve-year tenure as president from 1988 to 2000 (the last four as the first popularly elected president of the ROC), Lee made progress towards dismantling Taiwan's KMT party-state system. He nationalized the armed forces as part of an effort to reform state institutions to serve a government chosen by the people in competitive elections. From a military that was established in early twentieth-century China, saved by fleeing to Taiwan at mid-century, then rebuilt as an instrument for "reconquering the mainland," the ROC armed forces are today called upon to protect the people of Taiwan and their de facto sovereignty.

In achieving democracy, Taiwanese people have already liberated themselves from one Chinese dictatorship, one of the most repressive regimes of the post–World War II period. For Taiwanese aged thirty-five and younger, a democratic way of life is all they have ever known. As a result of democracy, it is now possible to advocate for a Taiwanese nation in speech, print, politics, art, and protest without fear of reprisal within Taiwan. Taiwanese identity has been unfettered since democratization. From 1992 to the present, the Election Study Center at National Chengchi University in Taipei has been asking respondents whether they consider themselves Taiwanese (*Taiwanren*台灣人), Chinese (*zhongguoren* 中國人), or both—and the percentage of respondents identifying as "Taiwanese only" has risen from 17.6% to 63.7%, while those identifying as "Chinese only" has fallen from 25.5% to 2.4%.[30]

There are asymptotic limits to what democracy can accomplish in Taiwan, however. Even the election of the first DPP president, Chen Shui-bian 陳水扁, in 2000, did not dismantle the ROC government or establish a new Republic of Taiwan. A Taiwanese nation aligned with

Taiwan's history and current contributions to the global economy remains incompletely built, still constrained by the legacy of the ROC and the aggression of the PRC. There was plenty of rhetoric in the 2020 election campaign suggesting that voters faced a binary, one-time choice between sovereignty and subjection. Yet national sovereignty exists in relation to other states in the international system. Without a paradigm shift in the goals and ideology of the CCP, or significantly stronger pledges of international support, the Taiwanese people cannot elect their way to an internationally recognized "Republic of Taiwan." The most they can do is try to evaluate, via the ballot box every two and four years, the best strategy—whether resistance, negotiation, or coerced cooperation—for preserving their democratic way of life. Choosing incorrectly could result in permanent losses. For now, deliverance—from invasion, annexation, or unwilling absorption—can only ever be conditional.

When President Tsai spoke of "The Republic of China (Taiwan)" in her victory speech to the crowd in Taipei at the beginning of 2020, her choice of words carried the burden of all this history, an acknowledgement of the tectonic geopolitical forces of US-China relations and the Taiwan "flashpoint" that stands between them in the early twenty-first century. For now, the formal adherence to the name "Republic of China (Taiwan)" holds those forces poised in a precarious balance.

Today, paradoxically, it is the People's Republic of China that is keeping the Republic of China in place. The existence of Two Chinas—the PRC and the ROC—is unacceptable to Beijing, but the primary target of its ire is Taiwanese self-determination. For Beijing, the PRC is the successor state to the ROC, the embodiment of Chinese historical progress, whereas a sovereign Taiwan is an offense against both this history and a hoped-for "Great Rejuvenation" of the Chinese nation. It rails continually against "Taiwanese independence forces" that might revise the ROC constitution to transform the "Republic of China (Taiwan)" into just "Taiwan." On New Year's Day 2019, CCP chairman Xi Jinping 習近平 warned in a major speech that if Taiwanese did not voluntarily accept their place in a unified China, then the CCP would make "no promise to abandon the use of force, and [would] retain the option of taking all necessary measures" to subordinate them. The Taiwanese people, he pledged, could keep their "private property, religious beliefs, and legitimate rights and interests" for an unspecified time—that is, until the CCP decided that they could be dispensed with.[31]

On October 9, 2021, the day before the 110th "National Day" of the Republic of China, Xi declared in a commemorative address that "the Chinese Communists are the most staunch supporters, most loyal collaborators, and most faithful successors of Mr. Sun Yat-sen's revolutionary cause, constantly realizing and developing the great ambitions of Mr. Sun Yat-sen and the pioneers of the 1911 [Xinhai] Revolution." Wang Yang, a Politburo member and chair of the commemoration, reiterated China's determination to "resolutely curb 'Taiwan independence' separatist activities and defend national sovereignty and territorial integrity."[32] The CCP shares with the hardline faction of today's KMT a belief that Taiwan and China are, or ought to be, part of one nation, even if they disagree over what political system or name that nation should have.[33] These erstwhile rivals also object to attempts—even informal or poorly informed ones—to associate the symbols of ROC sovereignty with a country called "Taiwan," such as treating the ROC National Day as a Taiwanese national day. At the same time, supporters of a Taiwanese republic also object to these attempts to equate the ROC with Taiwan, arguing that a true Taiwanese nation has yet to be founded.

Thus, the Republic of China endures as part of Beijing's efforts to prevent a nation called Taiwan from coming into being. The CCP reaches out to the KMT in strategic ways but expresses only monomaniacal opposition to the DPP. It rejects the right of Taiwanese people to engage in the democratic process itself, which can and does elect candidates from different parties to the legislature and executive as well as at the county and municipal levels. The result for the Taiwanese is living in a geopolitical hall of mirrors. The acknowledgment that Taiwan functions as an independent state separate from the PRC is met with threats of economic, diplomatic, and military retaliation by PRC officials. Increasingly, such threats are directed not only at the Taiwanese but also at public figures and even ordinary people from other countries who do not adhere to the double-speak and political fictions that help maintain the "status quo" of cross-Strait relations.

The whole world now lives in this refracted reality, too. Since 2019, politicians in former Eastern Bloc countries such as Lithuania, Estonia, and the Czech Republic have vocally defended Taiwanese democracy and worked to expand economic, cultural, and informal diplomatic ties with Taiwan.[34] In September 2020, Milos Vystrcil, president of the Czech Senate, visited Taiwan and gave a speech before the Legislative Yuan that echoed John F. Kennedy's Cold War–era *Ich bin ein Berliner* address. He drew parallels between Taiwan's contemporary resistance against the PRC and the struggle of Eastern European countries against the former Soviet Union. "Please allow me to express my support to the Taiwanese people in the same way," Vystrcil stated, before declaring: "I am a Taiwanese."[35] His words drew the predictable ire of CCP officials, who condemned his actions with the same angry language they regularly deploy against Taiwanese people. Beyond Vystrcil's rhetoric lay a deeper truth about contemporary geopolitics. When it comes to the pressure to adhere to Beijing's policies and attitudes on Taiwan, on some level, we are all Taiwanese.

VIRAL REALITIES: THE SUPPRESSION AND VISIBILITY OF TAIWAN TODAY

Recent global events shed light on how the functioning of the international system—partly premised on silencing and erasing Taiwan—is also impeded by Beijing's demand that all nation-states and multilateral organizations continue to abide by these dictates. Despite this, Taiwan has emerged ever more clearly as a society and polity with an identity that is distinct from both "China" and "the ROC." Some recent global events that have highlighted this are Taiwan's successful handling of the COVID-19 pandemic (despite its exclusion from the World Health Organization), its strategic importance especially in the Indo-Pacific region (due to increased PRC military pressure), and its critical role in global supply chains, particularly in semiconductor manufacturing.

Flanking Tsai Ing-wen on stage the night of her reelection on January 11, 2020, were William Lai 賴清德, then her incoming vice president and later the winner of the 2024 presidential election, and Chen Chien-jen 陳建仁, the outgoing vice president and a world-renowned epidemiologist who led Taiwan's fight against the Severe Acute Respiratory Syndrome (SARS) epidemic in 2003. The three of them were aware of what most in the crowd had not registered yet: that a novel coronavirus, which would come to be called SARS-CoV-2, had emerged in China, in the city of Wuhan. On election night in Taiwan, this imminent world pandemic registered only as rumors and passing news reports. Meanwhile, in Wuhan, a week of meetings of the Hubei provincial People's Congress and Party Congress was already in full swing, a series of gatherings that would come to be known in the new parlance as a "super-spreader" event.

Taiwanese public health officials, who had been keeping track of social media posts by Chinese whistleblowers, began screening flights from Wuhan at the end of December 2019. On January 13, 2020, a team of Taiwanese doctors visited Wuhan to observe the situation on the ground and reported back to Taipei on the 16th that the virus could be transmitted from human to human, three days before public confirmation by Chinese officials and six days before the World Health Organization.[36] The willingness of the DPP-led government to make decisions that could be said to prioritize public safety over CCP sentiments was evident when it defied WHO guidance (seemingly given to placate Chinese leadership) that travel restrictions were unnecessary and instead moved quickly to limit travel first from China and then the rest of the world.

Defying early predictions that it would be one of the places hardest hit by the novel coronavirus, just as it had been during SARS, Taiwan instead became a model of pandemic control. Excluded from the WHO, it was nonetheless one of only a handful of polities that managed to reduce domestic transmission of SARS-CoV-2 to zero for months on end (including an eight-month period between April and December of 2020). Its schools, offices, restaurants, and gathering spaces remained open, while much of the rest of the world locked down cities and people within their borders.[37] Amid the angry and divisive politics of COVID-19, especially in the US, the news from Taiwan seemed to come from a gentler, parallel dimension of human life. The headlines reported on the farewell concert held by the beloved 24-hour Eslite Dunnan bookstore in Taipei and the rockstar reception that Chen Shih-chung 陳時中, then Minister of Health, received when he visited the southern city of Tainan to promote domestic tourism, among many other examples of normal life continuing.[38]

During this period, Taiwan remained one of the most threatened places on Earth, yet also one of the freest, a rare place where ordinary life continued. Taiwan's long success at both keeping out SARS-CoV-2 and curtailing outbreaks when they did occur in 2020 and early 2021 revealed what had previously been hidden to many outside Taiwan: its exclusion from global organizations supposedly dedicated to peace and progress for all. Taiwan's COVID-19 policy also demonstrated that even informal diplomatic and humanitarian exchanges could alleviate this isolation, providing Taiwanese with a measure of support that PRC strategy under Xi Jinping is designed to make too costly to extend.

Even amid a burgeoning pandemic, Beijing remained focused on Taiwan's international representation. The WHO resorted to using increasingly bizarre terms in its reports to reconcile Beijing's ideological fixations with Taiwan's clearly separate pandemic management: "Taiwan, China," "Taipei Municipality," and even "Taipei and Environs."[39] In an interview with the Hong Kong broadcaster RTHK, Dr. Bruce Aylward, a Canadian epidemiologist and WHO advisor, gave an excruciating performance of this cognitive dissonance between geopolitics and viral realities. When asked about Taiwan's COVID-19 management, he first pleaded difficulty hearing, then hung up on the call. When the reporter dialed him in again, he had only this to say: "Well, we've already talked about China."[40] Soon after, Aylward's own profile was scrubbed from the WHO website, in an uncanny mimicry of its position on Taiwan.

Against the insistence that Taiwan is inseparable from China is the reality of the actions undertaken by the government in Taipei—enacting border closures for public safety and making decisions about how best to handle testing, quarantine, and treatment—all exercises in territoriality and sovereignty that are among the hallmarks of modern statehood. Moreover, the differential expressions of state power and sovereignty in China and Taiwan can be traced through their respective public health policies, practices, and technologies. For China, controlling the virus became a demonstration of overwhelming state power, characterized by massive lockdowns and a vast quarantine system. In contrast, the government in Taiwan emphasized transparency of information, with near-daily news conferences by the Central Epidemic Command Center (CECC, Zhihui Zhongxin 指揮中心). CECC announcements featured a canine "spokesperson" named Zongchai 總柴, sometimes rendered in cartoon form, whose smiling face exhorted an anxious public to comply with mask-wearing and quarantine regulations.[41] Taiwan's statism generally took the form not of awe-inspiring and intimidating control but of benign, familial inclusion and persuasion.

As the pandemic stretched into the summer and fall of 2020, and then into 2021, Taiwanese civil society and the Tsai administration leveraged it as an opportunity to strengthen preexisting ties and forge new ones by serving as both donors and recipients of international aid. Beginning in April 2020, the Taiwanese government donated 11 million surgical masks to the United States and eleven European countries, and 6 million masks to countries in Latin America and Southeast Asia, shipped in boxes stamped with the slogans "Taiwan Can Help" or "Love from Taiwan."[42] To reinforce the impact of these donations, nearly 27,000 Taiwanese people crowdfunded an advertisement that appeared in the April 14 print edition of the *New York Times*. It began: "In a time of isolation, we choose solidarity."[43] The message was that mutual care and coordination need not be limited by formal relations or lack thereof. Taiwan's "mask diplomacy" became a channel and pretext for humanitarian and diplomatic reciprocity, a material demonstration of Taiwan's statehood following in the path of the virus itself.

Taiwan experienced its first major outbreak of community spread of SARS-CoV-2 in May 2021, amidst a regional and global shortage of vaccines, when its vaccination rate against the virus was still at less than one percent.[44] A public that had been unusually united for a year since the election returned to a more typically fractious mean, divided over whether to implement strict lockdowns, test the population en masse, or accept the importation of Chinese-produced vaccines—essentially, to adopt the measures that the Chinese government had. Taiwan's vaccination campaign, and the domestic credibility of the Tsai administration, were saved by a series of vaccine donations by Japan and the United States— one, a former colonizer, and the other, its strongest unofficial ally—and also by former Eastern Bloc countries such as Lithuania, Poland, Slovakia, and the Czech Republic that had recently started to reach out to Taiwan.[45]

While the May 2021 outbreak came as a shock to the Taiwanese, who had grown accustomed to living in yet another state of exception during the pandemic—this time a biosocial one—its severity was limited compared to the crises sustained by many other nations in the same period. Almost alone among global societies, Taiwan prevented an outbreak that exceeded 1,000 confirmed cases a day until the spring of 2022, by which time over 76% of the population had received two or more doses of a COVID-19 vaccine.[46] On June 6, 2021, a bipartisan group of US Senators flew on a military plane to Taipei for a brief stopover to announce the donation of 750,000 vaccines (later more than tripled to 2.1 million doses).[47] The US State Department, under the administration of President Joseph Biden, reiterated that its commitment to Taiwan was "rock solid" and asserted that the US "maintains the capacity to resist any resort to force or other forms of coercion that would jeopardize the security or the social and economic system of the people on Taiwan."[48] Like the "mask diplomacy" of 2020, the vaccine donations of 2021 traced a new international reality for Taiwan in the wake of the virus. Taiwan was suddenly not so isolated.

These statements echoed the US commitment to "Free China" during the Cold War, when the US military had been activated on key occasions, such as the outbreak of the Korean War, to maintain Taiwan's separation from the PRC. Now, however, the "social and economic system of the people on Taiwan" was no longer authoritarian but liberal democratic, no longer in the hands of a dictator who saw the island as a means to the ends of his China dream, but in the hands of people who identified themselves as Taiwanese and saw their futures with one side of the Strait, not the other. The COVID-19 pandemic underscored not only Taiwan's anomalous status in the world order, which has prevailed for seven decades, but also how much has changed in the last generation—and so, too, what stands to be lost if Taiwan is taken control of against its will.

This book is a chronicle of Taiwan's struggles against two authoritarian Chinese governments—first, the party-state of the Republic of China from 1945 to the start of the democratic era in the mid-1990s and second, the party-state of the People's Republic of China today—and how the lessons from the first struggle have shaped and informed the second. It is also an examination of how a diverse group of people make sense of their experience of living on the fault lines of geopolitics, both at the center of US-China competition and on the margins of the post–World War II network of nation-states. Taiwan's isolation takes the form of denial—of membership, of a name, and of a voice. Yet Taiwan's predicament remains intractable not only because of Chinese nationalism and ambition but also because of Taiwanese agency and will. Taiwan has steadily resisted even when such resistance is silenced on the global stage at China's behest. Whether the early twenty-first century will merely prove to be a reprieve between rule by two dictatorships, the prelude to the establishment of a globally recognized Taiwanese state, or the continuation of a state of exception and ambiguity, remains to be seen. Taiwan is free today, as of the writing of this book; yet the question that structures life each day here is: How long will this freedom last?

NOTES

1. Central Election Commission, *2020 Presidential and Vice-Presidential Election*, January 21, 2020.
2. Stone Fish, "Stop Calling Taiwan a 'Renegade Province.'"
3. "China cleavage" is a term coined by the political scientist Nathan Batto. He writes, "To put it bluntly, you can understand most – somewhere between 70% and 90% – of Taiwan's politics if you understand the China Cleavage...Moreover, you can't understand anything else unless you understand how it is embedded within the China Cleavage." See Batto, "The NPP's internal divisions." The NPP is the abbreviation for the New Power Party.
4. Ko Wen-je 柯文哲, the former mayor of Taipei City, was the TPP's 2024 candidate for president, garnering more than a quarter of the votes cast in a three-way contest, at 26.5%. "Taiwan Election Live Results," *Bloomberg News*, January 13, 2024. On the nascent TPP-KMT legislative alliance, see Lai, "Reform or Overreach? Constitutional Controversies in Taiwan's Recent Legislative Changes".
5. Lin, "False information on the rise in Taiwan: academic"; and Wang, "Taiwan's Defenses Against Information Warfare Gain Attention." Examples include allegations that Tsai Ing-wen did not actually receive a PhD from the London School of Economics (LSE), akin to birtherism conspiracies against Barack Obama in the US.
6. Wong, "China's Latest Taiwan Tactic Closes the Door on Individual Holidays to the Island."
7. Rich, "Does it matter if Taiwan loses formal recognition?"
8. Ellis, "China Claims Diplomatic Coup over Taiwan with Solomon Switch.".
9. Rauhala, "'Reunification Is a Decision to Be Made By the People Here.'" The cover image depicted then presidential candidate Tsai Ing-wen of the DPP next to the headline, "She Could Lead The World's Only Chinese Democracy".
10. Mainland Affairs Council, "Public's View on Cross-Strait Relations."
11. The 2019 protests in Hong Kong have been the subject of multiple recent books that blend memoir, first-hand reporting, and academic study. See, for example, Wasserstrom, *Vigil: Hong Kong on the Brink*; Chan, *Aftershock: Essays from Hong Kong*; and Lim, *Indelible City*.

12. Tsai, "Full text of Taiwan President Tsai Ing-wen's acceptance speech."
13. For more on Taiwan's premodern history, see, for example, Shepherd, *Statecraft and Political Economy on the Taiwan Frontier, 1600–1800*; Andrade, *How Taiwan Became Chinese*; and Chiu, *The Colonial 'Civilizing Process' in Dutch Formosa, 1624–1662*.
14. For more on Qing Taiwan, see monographs including Teng, *Taiwan's Imagined Geography*, and Hung, *Shufan shehui wangle yu jiti yishi*.
15. For more on Japanese Taiwan, see academic work including Morris, *Japanese Taiwan* and Barclay, *Outcasts of Empire*.
16. Dawley, *Becoming Taiwanese*, 5–6.
17. "The Provisional Constitution of the Republic of China."
18. "Constitution of the Republic of China, October 10, 1923" and "Provisional Constitution of the Republic of China for the Period of Political Tutelage, June 1, 1931."
19. Carrai, *Sovereignty in China*, 124, 134.
20. For more on the immediate postwar era in Taiwan, see academic work including Phillips, *Between Assimilation and Independence*, as well as memoirs such as Peng, *A Taste of Freedom*, and Kerr, *Formosa Betrayed*.
21. For more, see Yang, *The Great Exodus*.
22. Ngo and Wang, *Politics of Difference in Taiwan*, 3.
23. For Taiwanese attempts to grapple with the enormity of the White Terror in art, literature, and film, see Lin, *Representing Atrocity in Taiwan*; Rowen, *Transitions in Taiwan*; and Goldblatt and Lin, *A Son of Taiwan*.
24. Yi-shen Chen, "'From a Province to a Sovereign State," 40–59.
25. For more on the process by which the ROC lost out on the title of the "real" China, without a recognized Taiwanese state emerging in its place, see Lin, *Accidental State*. For more on UN Resolution 2758 and the continued exclusion of Taiwanese people from effective representation in the UN, see Drun and Glaser, *The Distortion of UN Resolution 2758 and Limits on Taiwan's Access to the United Nations*.
26. For more on the democratization (*dangwai*) movement, see monographs including Rigger, *From Opposition to Power*; Jacobs, *Democratizing Taiwan*; and Sullivan and Nachman, *Taiwan*.
27. See Domes, "The 13th Party Congress of the Kuomintang," 356. "Finally, the platform outlines KMT policy towards the People's Republic of China. Although the chapter is entitled 'Mainland Recovery', significantly the hitherto vitriolic rhetoric used is superseded by somewhat anodyne statements about supporting 'political democratization', 'economic liberalization', 'social pluralism', and 'inspir[ing] cultural Sini-

cization', without, it should be noted, any explanation as to how these can be achieved".

28. "Additional Articles of the Constitution of the ROC," amended June 10, 2005, Laws and Regulations Database of the ROC (Taiwan), Ministry of Justice. As of August 2022, there are 12 Additional Articles. On March 25, 2022, the Legislative Yuan passed a proposed amendment to lower to voting age in general elections to 18 years of age. A national referendum will take place on November 26, 2022, to approve or reject the amendment.

29. "'New Constitution' means timetable for independence."

30. Election Study Center at National Chengchi University, *Taiwan/Chinese Identity (1992/06-2022/06)*.

31. Xi, "Working Together to Realize Rejuvenation of the Chinese Nation."

32. "Commemoration the 110th anniversary of the 1911 Revolution was held in Beijing."

33. For more on the 1992 Consensus (*jiuer gongshi*九二共識), the name given to a meeting between CCP and KMT officials before Taiwan democratized (during which attendees allegedly agreed that "there is only one China," with the KMT arguing that the meaning of "one China" is subject to "different interpretations"), see Drun, "Taiwan's Opposition Struggles to Shake Pro-China Image."

34. For more on deepening informal ties between Taiwan and former Eastern Bloc countries, see analysis including Stenberg, "'I am a Taiwanese.'"

35. Hille, "'I am a Taiwanese.'"

36. Smith, "Taiwanese official reveals China suspected 'human to human' transmission by January 13."

37. For more on Taiwan's success in containing Covid for much of 2020-early 2022, and the resulting implications for asserting sovereignty and drawing boundaries between Taiwan and China, see Wang, Ng, and Brook, "Response to Covid-19 in Taiwan," 1341–1342; Chou, "Island Utopia"; Rowen, "Crafting the Taiwan Model for Covid-19"; and Harrison, "Covid-19 Remapping East Asian Modernity."

38. Xie, "A 24-hour Bookstore Turns its Final Page"; and Lee, "Chen and team rock Tainan on visit."

39. World Health Organization, *Novel Coronavirus (2019-nCoV) Situation Report – 22*, February 11, 2020, 3.

40. Chan, "The WHO Ignores Taiwan. The World Pays the Price."

41. Hioe, "Between Infodemic and Pandemic."

42. Alton, "Taiwan's Covid-19 Response & 'Mask Diplomacy,'" 1–2.

43. "Crowdfunded 'Taiwan Can Help' ad published in New York Times," *Focus Taiwan (CNA English News)*, April 14, 2020.
44. Kuo and Chen, "Once a Covid success story, Taiwan struggles with a vaccine shortage."
45. Lin, "Dodging the Covid Bullet."
46. Records from Our World in Data, a project by the Global Change Data Lab and funded by Oxford University, and the Johns Hopkins Coronavirus Research Center, show that 76% of the population in Taiwan had received two doses of a Covid vaccine by March 24, 2022, the week that the original Omicron variant broke through the border quarantine. For more on the end of Taiwan's "Zero Covid" strategy, see Wei, "The Topsy-Turvy End of Zero Covid in Taiwan."
47. "US to donate 750,000 Covid vaccines to Taiwan: visiting senator," *Focus Taiwan (CNA English News)*, June 6, 2021.
48. United States Department of State, "Increasing People's Republic of China Military Pressure Against Taiwan Undermines Regional Peace and Stability"; and United States Department of State, Bureau of East Asian and Pacific Affairs, *US Relations with Taiwan Fact Sheet.*

CHAPTER 2

FOUR WAYS OF TELLING TAIWANESE HISTORY

A PILGRIMAGE TO TAINAN

Opened in October 2011, the National Museum of Taiwan History (NMTH, Guoli Taiwan lishi bowuguan 國立臺灣歷史博物館) is located not in the northern capital city of Taipei but in Tainan, in the southwest. Tainan is the oldest city on the island and the former capital, established in 1624 as a trading post by the Dutch East India Company (VOC) on the land of the indigenous Siraya people. In the wide forecourt to the entrance of the museum is a placid pond, incongruously meant to symbolize the Taiwan Strait, known as the "Black Ditch" to the settlers from China who made the treacherous crossing in the seventeenth to the nineteenth centuries. The main building looms large but low in the scorching southern Taiwan heat. Modernist in style, it combines architectural elements of a *siheyuan* 四合院, a traditional four-walled courtyard-style residence common among the most prosperous settlers, with the columns typical of stilt houses of indigenous Taiwanese nations, including the Kavalan and Truku.[1]

The location of the museum—next to an estuary that filled up with silt in the eighteenth century, ending its utility as a channel for foreign trade—is a recognition both to the longer arc of Taiwan's history and one reason why this same history remains so hidden to outside observers. A tourist who wanted to make a visit to the museum after landing at Taoyuan International Airport, forty minutes outside of Taipei, would first have to take the two-hour high-speed rail from the city of Taoyuan to Tainan, then a local train, followed by an infrequent bus or else a long taxi ride to far outside the city center. Small wonder perhaps that it is nowhere to be found on any customary tourist itinerary.

The authorization in 1999 of a taxpayer-funded museum focused specifically on the history of Taiwan and its inhabitants was a sign of how quickly politics and identity had shifted after Taiwan democratized in the late 1980s and early 1990s. The "nation" referred to in the name "National Museum" was technically the Republic of China (ROC), yet by the early twenty-first century, Taiwan (the colony) had in some respects begun to displace the metropole.

The NMTH opened in October 2011 at a conjuncture, two decades into what began as a fragile, contested move towards democracy in Taiwan, and as the new "Chinese Century" of PRC geopolitical and economic dominance was unfolding. At a press conference to celebrate the opening, the new director Lu Li-cheng 呂理政 declared, "We will present the history of the Taiwanese people in a museum designed for them." The simplicity of this statement belied the boldness of the claim that "Taiwan history" and "Taiwanese people" existed as categories that could be documented and displayed in a museum. It implicitly referenced a decades-long political struggle that had made it possible to make such a speech in public without fear. Lu drew a contrast between the NMTH, the first major public museum to bring together "both history and Taiwan," and the renowned National Palace Museum (NPM, Guoli gugong bowuguan 國立故宮博物館).[2] A standard itinerary stop for tourists and foreign dignitaries for decades, the NPM was built by the KMT in 1965 to house more than 700,000 artifacts from Chinese imperial history that the Nationalists had taken with them during their flight across the Strait. Unlike the NPM, which was intended to buttress the illusion that Taiwan was the "real China," safe from the cultural destruction of the Chinese Communist Party, the NMTH was built on the premise that Chinese history was just one part of a Taiwanese history that long predated the arrival of the ROC. The story of modern Taiwan, NTMH officials argue, is the journey of the Taiwanese people to learn about their multiple histories of colonialism and liberation and ultimately to push back against the geopolitics of the international system itself.

Taiwan's contested geopolitical status today is premised in part on the fallacy that Taiwanese history and Chinese history are contiguous. The year 1949, when the KMT was defeated in the Chinese Civil War and moved the government of the ROC to Taipei along with an estimated 1.2 million soldiers and refugees, was also the year Taiwan was press-ganged into a contest between the KMT and the CCP over who would build, claim, and govern a "reunified" Chinese nation. Aside from Taiwan and close outlying islands like the Pescadores and Green Island, the only other significant portion of ROC land the KMT retained control over were the island groups of Kinmen and Matsu, lying just kilometers away from to the southeastern coast of Fujian Province in China. Two realities, that of Taiwan and the ROC, thus came to occupy the same territory.

The emphasis on the events of 1949 and the idea of a China still divided between the Communists and the Nationalists lead to highly contradictory, even nonsensical, characterizations of Taiwan: as a place without history before the mid-twentieth century and yet somehow also historically an inalienable part of China right up to that point. This perspective fails to account for the persistent statements by indigenous nations and long-term settlers, and even plenty of third-generation descendants of 1949-era refugees from China, that this is a country unto itself, official titles notwithstanding. It fails to account, in other words, for why Taiwan has become a geopolitical problem in the first place—why, if it is "really Chinese," if the separation with China has supposedly been so recent, neither deep economic integration nor diplomatic or military coercion from across the Strait have dissolved the division.

In this chapter, we take the reader through a virtual visit of the NMTH while presenting four alternative stories about Taiwan that explain how it came to be a de facto independent state with a collective identity and way of life that differs significantly from that of modern China. Each of these narratives offers an atypical periodization that shows the reader how to think about Taiwan outside of the 1949 framework: as a serial settler colony that has yet to be decolonized; as the site of a century-long struggle for self-determination that predates the existence of either the ROC or PRC; as a territory that has already undergone unification with China (the ROC) once in the modern age, a chaotic and repressive experience for those who lived through it; and as a place that is routinely denied the right to tell its own history or shape its own future.

First is Taiwan's history as an indigenous homeland repeatedly colonized by outsiders and outside powers, producing a majority Han Chinese population through settlement, dispossession, intermarriage, and forced assimilation. For approximately six thousand years, indigenous Austronesian-language peoples have called the island home. The indigenous groups of the southwest coastal plains encountered European empires at roughly the same time as indigenous peoples in the present-day United States, Canada, New Zealand, and Australia did. The uniqueness of Taiwan's story, compared to these former British colonies, is that it was then incorporated into two Asian empires, firstly Qing China (as a prefecture from 1683 to 1885, and then as part of the new Fukien-Taiwan Province from 1885 to 1895) and then into Imperial Japan (from 1895 to 1945).

The second story is Taiwan's century-long movement for democracy and autonomy, which preceded the establishment of either of the two modern Chinese nation-states. In 2021, Taiwan celebrated the centennial of two such movements launched during Japanese colonialism, the Taiwan Cultural Association (Taiwan wenhua xiehui 台灣文化協會) and the

League for the Establishment of a Taiwanese Parliament (Taiwan yihui shezhi qingyuan yundong 台灣議會設置請願運動). These anniversaries stand against attempts to fold Taiwan into rigidly Chinese narratives, whether the 72 years since the KMT fled across the Strait, or the 110 years since the founding of the ROC. Today, Taiwanese academics, politicians, and activists increasingly recognize the 1920s as the start of modern Taiwanese consciousness and desire for self-rule.

The third story is Taiwan's earlier attempted unification with China. This history begins with the surrender of Taiwan by Japan in 1945 and the occupation of the island by the KMT. The people of Taiwan had been handed from one brutal colonial master to another without the right of self-determination. Tensions between "mainlanders" and Taiwanese, and the mismanagement and corruption of the new regime, led to the 228 Incident (Ererba shijian 二二八事件) that began on February 28, 1947. In response to ensuing protests against KMT rule, ROC troops killed an estimated 20,000 Taiwanese in retaliation. The trauma of the killings and the thirty-eight years of martial law that followed have since shaped the logic and tenacity of Taiwan's resistance to yet another Chinese authoritarian government, the PRC. "Reunification" is often framed as a possible outcome for Taiwan in the future, but it has already been tried once, with disastrous results for the Taiwanese.

The fourth story is Taiwan's future as a polity potentially living on borrowed time. Taiwan's trajectory also intersects with that of Xinjiang, Tibet, and Hong Kong, all borderlands that, like it, were once incorporated into the Qing Empire but, unlike Taiwan, are today governed as part of the PRC. Xi Jinping, the chairman of the Chinese Communist Party, has held Hong Kong up as a model for what should happen to Taiwan, once its people are subdued and "reeducated." The last part of what a post-unification future will entail is sometimes spoken, sometimes not. Each day, the people of Taiwan struggle instead to write a different future than the one Chinese officials are trying to script for them.

ONE: INDIGENOUS HOMELANDS

In the late sixteenth century, as Portugal began constructing a far-flung maritime empire, a crew of Portuguese sailors became the first Europeans to pass by Taiwan. They gave Taiwan the name "Ilha Formosa" (beautiful island) the term by which Taiwan was most popularly known in the Western world until the middle of the twentieth century. Looking at Taiwan from this vantage point, what becomes apparent is not its inseparability from China but how much its history resembles in key ways that of New World nation-states like the United States, Canada, Australia, and New Zealand. Taiwan was also a settler colony, a site on which European powers competed for territory and commodities with devastating consequences for the original inhabitants. The main exhibit at the NMTH begins the story here, describing Taiwan before the 1620s as a "free island uncontrolled by any regime" and identifying the early years of colonialism as the dividing line between the island's prehistory and history.[3]

Today, 95% of citizens in Taiwan trace much of their ancestry across the Strait—a minority from the KMT retreat in 1949 (approximately 10–13%) and a majority from settlement in the eighteenth through the early twentieth centuries. The demographics of modern Taiwan are not natural or ancient any more than Australia or New Zealand's predominantly Anglo populations.[4] Instead, the composition of Taiwan's population is the result of global historical forces.

Beginning in 1568, the Protestant northern provinces of the Netherlands revolted against their Spanish Catholic Habsburg princes, in what became known as the Eighty Years' War. A succession crisis in Portugal in 1580 brought both the kingdom itself and its burgeoning overseas empire under Spanish Habsburg rule until 1640. Dutch and Spanish conflict was externalized, in the form of mutual piracy and competitive colonialism, far beyond the boundaries of continental Europe, eventually reaching Taiwan. In 1571, Spanish explorers seized the city of Manila on the island of Luzon, inaugurating the trans-Pacific galleon trade and transporting silver from Mexican mines to meet surging demand in Ming-dynasty China. For their part, the Dutch began their forays into Southeast Asia with the incorporation of the VOC in 1602 and the establishment of trading posts at Bantam in 1603 and Batavia in 1611, in addition to opening trade with Tokugawa Japan in 1609.

After multiple failed attempts to force the Ming to allow them to set up a port in Fujian, and an unsuccessful attack on Portuguese-controlled Macau in 1622, the VOC occupied the Pescadores (Penghu), an archipelago thirty miles off the western coast of Taiwan. They continued carrying out raiding operations on the Chinese coast until they were expelled by a Ming fleet in 1624. Thereafter, they moved to Taiwan, which the Ming did not claim to hold, and built a settlement called Fort Zeelandia on the southwestern coast in the town of Anping, now part of the city of Tainan. In 1626, the Spanish established their own rival colony in the north of the island, in what is now the port city of Keelung, with the intention of protecting the Manila trade from Dutch interference.

As European empires jockeyed for regional domination, Taiwan remained home to more than a dozen linguistically and culturally diverse indigenous peoples whose history on the island stretched back for more than 5,000 years.[5] Together, they numbered approximately 100,000 people in the early seventeenth century.[6] The geographic and chronological progression of colonialism in Taiwan, starting from the southwest and northwest in the early seventeenth century and stretching into the Central Mountain Range and the east coast in the nineteenth and twentieth centuries, meant that different indigenous peoples experienced land loss, conflict with outsiders, intermarriage, and assimilation in different environmental and ecological contexts and at different periods in Taiwanese history.

The Siraya were the first indigenous communities to encounter colonizers. At their arrival, the Dutch relied on Siraya villages for shelter and survival and worked to win their alliance through gift-giving and ceremony. Siraya languages served as a lingua franca for the area until the end of the 1800s. The Dutch quickly became embroiled in frequent intra-Siraya conflict and subsequently faced a major uprising by the villages of Mattauw and Bacaluan beginning in the summer of 1629, which they put down through a series of "punitive expeditions."[7] The Dutch viewed the 1635 Mattauw Treaty as creating a relationship of vassalage and overlordship between Siraya villages and the VOC. Indigenous representatives today, however, dispute that the Siraya signatories intended to or did relinquish their claims to sovereignty.

As the historian Tonio Andrade outlines, the goal of Dutch merchants and troops was to extract profit from their new colony by importing semi-indentured laborers, who comprised the first large-scale settlement of people from southeast China to Taiwan. In a process he labeled "co-colonization," the VOC attracted farmers from Ming China with pledges of land and special licenses. This was a Dutch colony on Siraya land, worked by Chinese settlers who planted rice and sugar and hunted sika deer pelts that the VOC then taxed or sold to China and Japan.[8] At the time of the Dutch arrival in 1624, an estimated 1,500 Han Chinese fishermen and traders from Fujian were also residing in Taiwan. By the end of Dutch governance in the area nearly four decades later, that number had increased to about 30,000 to 50,000.[9]

Sinicization, consisting of successive waves of Han Chinese settlement, aspiring rulers and empires arriving from China, and Sinitic languages that came to predominate over Austronesian ones, is the primary form of colonization that has taken place in Taiwan. Although the Dutch succeeded in dislodging the Spanish from the north of Taiwan in 1648, they were unable to hold off an invasion in 1661 by Koxinga, the Ming loyalist military leader. As Chiang Kai-shek and the KMT would do nearly three centuries later while retreating from the CCP, Koxinga and his forces occupied southwestern Taiwan while retreating from the advancing Manchus, hoping initially to use it as a base to restore Ming rule in China. His short-lived Kingdom of Tungning, which was centered in Anping, similar to Dutch Taiwan, marked the first time that any part of the island was governed by a Chinese ruler. It was not until the Qing defeated Koxinga's grandson Zheng Keshuang 鄭克塽 in 1683 that any portion of Taiwan was governed by the same regime holding power in China.

At this point, as visitors to the NMTH learn, "Taiwan was transformed from an open maritime trading post to a place of little importance on the frontiers of the [Qing] empire. The permanent exhibit describes Taiwan in this period as "mov[ing] away from the era of international trade, entering instead an era of agricultural development led by migrants from China's Fujian and Guangdong provinces."[10] This era would last for two hundred years, until the Qing ceded Taiwan to Japan in 1895, as part of the Treaty of Shimonoseki that concluded the first Sino-Japanese war.

Qing rule in Taiwan shared key features with British and French imperialism in the eighteenth and nineteenth centuries, at times offering support for colonists and at others trying to restrain them, both from encroaching further on indigenous land and from rebelling against metropolitan authorities.[11] The Qing empire mostly grew west into central and south Asia—into Xinjiang and Tibet—but the Han Chinese population also increased on its eastern frontier, in Taiwan. As James Millward, one of the leading historians of the school of thought known as "New Qing History" notes, in "the territories newly acquired by the Qing, Han settler colonialism followed wherever farming was environmentally feasible." In practice, this meant seizing or purchasing land from indigenous populations. By the very early twentieth century, there were nearly 2.9 million people from China or descended from Chinese settlers living in Taiwan, living far beyond the boundaries of the original Dutch and Spanish colonies.[12] In Taiwan, Qing officials ultimately claimed about forty percent of the island, stretching from part of the Hengchun Peninsula and curving around the western coast and up around the northern end of the island, ending approximately at the modern city of Yilan. Millward continues: "These places were not 'open', nor were they 'wilderness' any more than the pre-Columbian Americas were."[13]

Despite being an early modern and modern phenomenon, mass Chinese settlement in Taiwan during the Qing dynasty is often used by Beijing to assert that Taiwan is naturally a part of China and that any other political configuration in the present day is an aberration. Such teleologies are based on a belief that Qing military and administrative expansion constitutes not imperialism in the vein of European empires, but rather the filling out of an always existing and inseparable nation, the far borders of which should be taken as the rightful territory of any Chinese nation henceforth.

The "retrocession" of Taiwan from Japan to the forty-four-year-old Republic of China in 1945 is often characterized as a return to an essential, eternal Chinese nation, hiding the colonial features of this new era of governance. Like the Japanese before them, the KMT uprooted villages, banned indigenous languages from schools, and pushed traditionally mobile tribes to engage in sedentary agriculture. After their defeat in 1949, in short order, they settled over a million soldiers and refugees from China on Taiwanese soil, hastily constructing military villages (*juancun* 眷村) to house poorer servicemen and their dependents. The KMT also initiated state-building projects in eastern and mountain indigenous communities that had only come under centralized state governance during the Japanese era, supplying food, services, and infrastructure under its version of a Leninist party-state system.[14]

The new regime invented the term—*pingdi shanbao ji shandi shanbao* 平地山胞及山地山胞, literally translated as "lowland and highland mountain compatriots"—to refer to indigenous Taiwanese.[15] As Awi Mona (Chi-wei Tsai) explains, the

> ROC government considered "*shanbao*" as "citizens of distinctive lifestyles" who were inferior in essence...Initially, indigenous land administration under [the] ROC continued former Japanese land management systems, declared indigenous lands as national land through the power of eminent domain, and had taken land from indigenous peoples without compensation.[16]

The designation "*shanbao*" became the basis for a system that the anthropologist Scott Simon describes as "bifurcated citizenship," which doled out variable treatment to indigenous and non-indigenous citizens.[17] As Simon explains, the KMT "cultivated a local political elite, maintaining 'mountain compatriots' as a distinct legal category important for land policy and electoral politics."[18] As part of the KMT's early political coalition-building, indigenous Taiwanese were allocated seats in local councils from the 1950s. They were also allocated seats in the national legislature beginning in the 1970s, when so-called "supplementary elections" were held to replace the thinning ranks of those KMT members who had been elected on the mainland in 1948 and died in Taiwan. By the time the Additional Articles of the ROC Constitution were passed in 1991, after the end of martial law, there were eight legislative seats reserved for indigenous Taiwanese, four each for "lowland" and "highland" groups. Further reform in 2006 halved the total size of the legislature to 113 members and indigenous seats to six.[19]

Due to the efforts of activists from the 1970s onwards, the wording in the Additional Articles referring to indigenous Taiwanese was changed in 1994 to "the original inhabitants of the lowlands and highlands" (*pingdi yuanzhumin ji shandi yuanzhumin* 平地原住民及山地原住民).[20] The term *yuanzhumin* 原住民 was meant to indicate that indigenous Taiwanese were not merely one ethnic group within the ROC but rather the first inhabitants of the land to which the ROC government had relocated. Sixteen indigenous nations are now legally recognized in Taiwan. By contrast, the PRC constitution does not include the category of indigeneity at all, only "ethnic minorities" (*shaoshu minzu* 少數民族). The PRC classifies all indigenous Taiwanese into a single ethnic minority it calls "high mountain peoples" (*gaoshan minzu* 高山民族).[21]

In another landmark moment, on August 1, 2016, President Tsai Ing-wen, whose maternal grandmother was Paiwan indigenous, delivered the first-ever apology by the ROC government to indigenous Taiwanese. Her speech was notable for the way it rewrote Taiwanese history as one of indigenous subjugation by successive groups of settlers, a feature that remained consistent regardless of which foreign regime—Dutch, Spanish, Zheng, Qing, Japanese, or ROC—was then in place. "Four hundred years ago, there were already people living in Taiwan," she said. "But then, without their consent, another group of people arrived on their shores, and in the course of history took everything from the first inhabitants, who on the land they have known most intimately became...foreign, out of the mainstream, and marginalized."[22] Tsai's apology echoed those made to the First Nations of Australia and Canada in 2008 by the governments of both countries, part of a global reckoning of colonial violence and indigenous dispossession.[23]

In this version of the Taiwan story, it becomes clear why the modern movement for indigenous rights has not always aligned with aspirations for "Taiwan independence" and the focus on China-Taiwan relations that structures it. Taiwan's contested status makes its premodern history especially prone to instrumentalization. As sociologist Mark Munster-hjelm notes, arguments supporting a new Taiwanese nation frequently treat indigenous peoples as "living dead"—valued for their genetic and cultural links to a pre-Sinophone Taiwan but discriminated against today and made to serve political ends that are not necessarily of their choosing.[24] Issues, such as language revitalization, economic opportunity, hunting rights, and land restoration, that are often the most important to indigenous tribes can potentially be pursued within the existing constitutional framework. They also often highlight the limitations of the unitary nation-state altogether. As political scientist Ek-hong Ljavakaw Sia has explained, the goal of indigenous Taiwanese is often "autonomism" and "self-rule, rather than outright national independence...[not] secession from the state [but for it] to recognize, respect strengthen, and support aborigines in accordance with their requirements and needs...and their sustainable development."[25]

Such an arrangement might take a number of forms. For example, in 1999, representatives from eleven recognized indigenous tribes presented

Chen Shui-bian, then the DPP candidate for president, with a document that came to be called the "New Partnership Between the Government of Taiwan and Aboriginal Nations" (Yuanzhuminzu yu Taiwanzhengfu xin de huoban guanxi 原住民族與台灣政府新的夥伴關係). Chen signed it in a ceremony on Orchid Island, the island off the southeast coast of Taiwan that is home to the Tao nation. With this, the DPP also became the first political party in Taiwan "to proactively define a policy on indigenous rights."[26] The first, second, and third sections of the document, respectively, "recognize the natural sovereignty of Taiwan's indigenous peoples" and direct the government to "promote their autonomy" and to "conclude land treaties with [them]," articulating what Chun-chi Hung has called a vision of "parallel sovereignty."[27] In 2002, in his first term as president, Chen reaffirmed the New Partnership, the first time that an ROC president had "clearly proclaimed that indigenous peoples are this land of Taiwan's original masters, and their natural sovereignty takes precedence over that of the state."[28] The speech itself was titled "A State within a State" (*Guo zhong you guo* 國中有國) and repeated a statement Chen had made during a televised debate during his reelection campaign expressing his hope for a new constitution in which the "New Partnership" and its principles of a "state within a state" and "quasi-nation-to-nation relations" (*zhun guo yu guo guanxi* 準國與國關係) would form the basis of a special constitutional chapter on indigenous peoples.[29] Chen's call for constitutional reform that would acknowledge indigenous Taiwanese more explicitly was promptly condemned by CCP officials as being a call for Taiwanese independence in disguise. Such proposals also met strong resistance from the administration of US president George W. Bush.

Although Chen's push for a new constitution failed and the "New Partnership" was never ratified, it was under his tenure that the 2005 Indigenous People's Basic Law (Yuanzhuminzu jibenfa 原住民族基本法) was passed, the result of years of lobbying and organizing by indigenous rights' groups. Article Four commits the government to "guarantee[ing] the equal status and development of self-governance of indigenous peoples," while Article Five states that "The state shall provide sufficient resources and allocate abundant annual budget to assist indigenous peoples in developing autonomy."[30] Yet implementation of the law has fallen far short. The contemporary political realities for Taiwan's indigenous groups exhibit a familiar tension between a stated commitment to reconciliation and transitional justice on the one hand, and the political and economic interests of the majority settler group on the other. Expansive gestures towards rectifying past injustice transform at ground level into more pointed and discomforting debates about land rights, education, affirmative action, and welfare policy.

Two recent examples illustrate how halting and contested decolonization is in practice. The first is the effort of Siraya activists to gain recognition from the central government. At the writing of this book, only two categories of indigenous peoples, the "highland" and "lowland" tribes of the central mountains, East Rift Valley, eastern and southeastern coasts, are named in the ROC constitution. "Plains indigenous" (*pingpuzu* 平埔族), the name given to peoples like the Siraya who lived on the western plains, have been left out. Indigenous status was itself a product of colonization, a way for successive empires and governments to categorize and manage different populations. Today it is also used by the ROC to distribute limited amounts of political power, financial resources, and social benefits, thus making the question of who qualifies as sufficiently indigenous (based on heritage, tribe, community affinity, linguistic proficiency, naming practices, or state- or self-identity) a fraught one.

Siraya campaigners have met with resistance both from the state and from members of formally recognized tribes whose ancestors experienced the full impact of colonialism and outside settlement later in Taiwan's history. In June 2022, a group of Amis, Paiwan, and Puyuma councilors in Taitung issued a statement opposing inclusion of the Siraya under the Status Act for Indigenous Peoples (Yuanzhumin shenfenfa 原住民身分法). The Amis (or Pangcah) and the Paiwan are, respectively, the two largest recognized indigenous groups today, with officially declared populations of 213,514 and 102,730 as of January 2020. They were among the last to be seriously impacted by colonialism, beginning in the twilight of Qing rule on the island. Taitung County Council Deputy Speaker Lin Tsung-han 林琮翰 warned that counting the Siraya might mean that "Taiwan's indigenous people would soon disappear due to Sinicization."[31] The Siraya may number up to a million, whereas the current number of recognized indigenous is only 580,000 total. The logic, as the scholar Jolan Hsieh (also known by her Siraya name Bavaragh Dagalomi) argues, is that if the Siraya, who are often construed as having been "'completely Sinicized' through assimilation into Han society," are accorded state sanction for their self-identification as indigenous, then the meaning of indigeneity in Taiwan will be diluted.[32]

The second example is the fitful effort to restore indigenous land rights. On February 14, 2017, the Council of Indigenous Peoples (CIP, Yuanzhuminzu weiyuanhui 原住民族委員會), a ministry of the executive branch, announced draft regulations declaring 800,000 hectares of land to be traditional tribal territory, the development of which must be carried out with the input of indigenous communities. Icyang Parod, the head of the CIP and a member of the Amis tribe, celebrated the proposals as a first step in "restor[ing] land justice to indigenous peoples" and stated that the government would press ahead with confirming them despite vociferous criticism that the survey methods excluded privately held land, thus undercounting tribal territory by one million hectares.[33]

In response, a group of activists launched a seven-year-long protest, spearheaded by the Puyuma-Amis singer Panai Kusui, her husband, the Bunun musician Nabu Husungan Istanda, and the Amis documentary filmmaker Mayaw Biho, demanding that use of indigenous territory now under private ownership also be subject to the same standards of tribal involvement and oversight. They began their protest on February 23, 2017, on Ketagalan Boulevard in Taipei, the street directly in front of the Presidential Palace, which was once known as Chieh Shou Road 介壽路, or "Long Live Chiang Kai-shek Road" before it was renamed in

1996 to honor the plains indigenous people who made their home in the Taipei Basin.[34] Panai's encampment was dismantled multiple times by city authorities and shuffled around to other parts of Zhongzheng district.[35] For more than 1,000 days, it was located at the 228 Peace Park (Ererba heping gongyuan 二二八和平公園), built to honor the victims of the February 28th, 1947 Incident.

One of the protest's slogans—"No one is an outsider" (*meiyou ren shi juwairen* 沒有人是局外人)—was meant to build solidarity between indigenous and Han Taiwanese living together on the same land. Yet despite holding performances, teach-ins, and rallies, generating media coverage, and hosting environmental activists and young politicians from the DPP and the recently established New Power Party (NPP, Shidai liliang 時代力量), the organizers did not manage to grow their encampment into a mass occupation or a more broad-based social movement.[36] Indigenous Taiwanese were also divided over the feasibility of the protesters' demands and the issues they chose to prioritize. Situated in a corner of the Peace Park, less visible than its previous iteration on Ketagalan Boulevard, the encampment was easy to miss, especially when it was unmanned. Under its white tent was a sign counting the number of days the protest had lasted and several large posters, including one of Panai performing at Tsai Ing-wen's first inauguration in May 2016, with the character *pian* 騙, or "liar," written over the image of the president.

Still, in Taiwan, the challenge of a prospective takeover by the PRC has created space to confront, however imperfectly, the legacy of Han settler colonialism. This is a public discursive space that currently does not exist in the Xinjiang or Tibetan Autonomous Regions, which were militarily annexed by the PRC in 1949 and 1950, and where Tibetan and Uyghur languages, religion, and culture are the subject of mandatory Sinicization and secularization campaigns by the state.[37] Just as indigenous voices are heard more clearly domestically in a democratic Taiwan, they are also heard speaking internationally against a PRC takeover. In January 2019, representatives from the Indigenous Historical Justice and Transitional

Justice Committee (Yuanzhuminzu lishizhengyi yu zhuanxingzhengyi liweiyuan 原住民族歷史正義與轉型正義委員會) responded to a New Year's speech by Xi Jinping warning Taiwan that it must accept "one country, two systems" with their own narrative of Taiwan's history and will to resist.[38] Speaking as a collective, the letter-writers, drawn from each of the sixteen recognized tribes and two unrecognized plains tribes from the north and south, pointed out that since the seventeenth century, indigenous Taiwanese had interacted with foreign powers as nations in their own right. "We signed contracts with the Dutch and peace agreements with the Americans," they wrote. "We have fought against imperialism and every foreign intruder on our land."[39]

The letter drew subtle attention to how long most of the land in Taiwan remained under the control of indigenous tribes, well into the latter days of Qing tenure on the western half of the island. The "peace agreement" referenced was the Nanjia Treaty signed in the aftermath of the Rover Incident of March 1867, when members of the Paiwan nation killed the surviving crew of a shipwrecked American vessel. This sparked a retaliatory venture. Qing Chinese officials in Tainan disclaimed responsibility by telling Charles William Le Gendre, the American consul at Amoy (Xiamen) in Fujian, that Paiwan lands, located in the mountains and coastal plains of the southeastern portion of the island, lay beyond their jurisdiction. Le Gendre personally led a second mission in July, cutting deep into Paiwan territory to negotiate a treaty with the chief Tok-a-Tok, who united eighteen tribes under his rule, to guarantee the safety of future American and European sailors who might wash up on his shores.[40]

The letter continued, "No government, no political party, no organization has the right to negotiate with any foreign power in an attempt to surrender the control of our traditional territory. We are the determined guardians of our motherland, as we have been for thousands of years and will continue to be." The letter portrayed Taiwan not as a single entity that could be granted wholesale to the Chinese government but as an

island made up of separate indigenous territories, none of which could
be relinquished without permission of the tribe that calls it home. In this
narrative, the seventeenth century marked the start of the colonial era
but also the beginning of an unbroken history of indigenous resistance,
with this rebuttal to Xi forming the latest example. "It is true that we are
not satisfied with the current [ROC] government of Taiwan, the sovereign state that has been built upon our motherland," the commissioners
wrote. "Nevertheless, Taiwan is also a nation that we are striving to build
together with other peoples who recognize the distinct identity of this
land...We do not share the monoculturalism, unification, and hegemony
promoted by...the government of China...It is of nothing that we desire."[41]

Two: A CENTURY OF TAIWANESE IDENTITY

The story of Taiwan's indigenous nations, both in the past and the
present, is occluded by the geopolitical forces that have shaped the
twentieth century. It is one of the multiple versions of Taiwan that
Taiwanese people contend with that remain difficult to highlight outside
of the island. The common habit of international observers of starting
the Taiwan story in 1949, with the split between the Nationalists and
the Communists forcing Taiwan into a Cold War matrix, entirely misses
the role of early modern settler colonialism in shaping the cultures and
societies of Taiwan. It also misses by more than a generation the first
conquest of the eastern portion of the island by a foreign power, the
Japanese Government-General, as well as the early development of a
Taiwanese identity, and with it, demands for autonomy by the people
who came to see their destinies as tied up with the island and its place
in the wider world.

The Japanese era began with the declaration of the only Republic
of Taiwan to ever exist on more than just paper.[42] On April 17, 1895,
the Qing government signed over Taiwan to Japan in the Treaty of
Shimonoseki. This, however, was a fate that many Taiwanese would not
accept. Two days later, Tang Jingsong 唐景崧, the Qing Governor of

Taiwan, summoned the British Consul Lionel Charles Hopkins to his Taipei compound. Hopkins arrived from his home in the nearby port town of Tamsui the next day to find a deputation waiting to present him with an unusual petition. "The population of the whole of Formosa are not willing to belong to Japan," it began, imploring "Great Britain [to] protect the territory and inhabitants of Formosa" in exchange for trade duties from the considerable natural resources of the island, including "gold, coal, sulfur, camphor, and tea."[43] Hopkins's superiors turned down the request. As the Qing representatives stationed on the island faced the impending cessation of their authority, and panic rose among the populace, Tang claimed to have received advice from a French naval commander passing through that "the French would offer assistance if Formosa seeks independence."[44] Thus, on May 23, the Republic of Formosa (Taiwanminzhuguo 台灣民主國) was proclaimed with Tang as its first president.

The Chinese-language text of the Republic's foundational declaration is lost, but American writer and trader James W. Davidson recorded a translation. It repeated the contention that the "Foreign Powers…aver that the People of Formosa must establish their independence before the Powers will assist them." Tang and the "men of respectability" who stood with him expressed their aspiration to "convert the whole island of Formosa into a Republican State," with "the administration of all our state affairs [to be] organized and carried on by the deliberations and decisions of Officers publicly elected by us the people."[45] While Davidson's text used the term "independence," Tang spoke instead of "self-governance" (zizhi自治) and used the phrase "yong Qing" (永清), meaning "Eternal Qing," to describe his tenure in office, suggesting that he did not intend for the new Republic to challenge Qing rights to Taiwan.[46] Still, the Republic's supporters did what they could to invest it with the trappings of nationhood during its brief life. They announced the establishment of a bicameral legislature and a cabinet with positions for ministers of war, and foreign and domestic affairs. They designed a Great Seal for official documents, as well as postage stamps for correspondence.[47] Replicas of the Republic's striking double-sided flag—featuring a stylized tiger with its head curved upwards against a blue backdrop—hang today in the NMTH in Tainan and the National Taiwan Museum in Taipei. Despite these efforts, no aid from the French was forthcoming. On June 6, Tang fled from the Republic he had so briefly led, back to China. Upon their arrival soon thereafter, Japanese troops managed to put down the initial armed resistance, moving north to south along the western coast and taking the last major city, Tainan, on October 21.

Established in response to an unforeseen exigency, the Republic of Formosa prefigured the articulation of a modern, island-wide Taiwanese identity, showing how people in Taiwan understood and participated in a broader trend of aspiring towards nationhood in the age of empire. In the fleeting life of this late nineteenth-century Republic we find recurring elements of the Taiwan story today: the negotiation by great powers for the island, the attempt by Taiwanese to internationalize their plight and prove their value to the global economy, and the predication of assistance by would-be allies on either clarifying Taiwan's geopolitical status or keeping it ambiguous.

The new Japanese regime, the Government-General (*Sōtoku-fu* 総督府), was intent upon harnessing and exploiting the human and natural resources of the island with more rigor than the Qing had been capable of. As Paul R. Katz has argued, the armed resistance of people in Taiwan after 1895 is not reducible to expressions of nationalism, whether pro-ROC or proto-Taiwanese; rather it can be analyzed in a comparative context "as one variant of a global phenomenon, namely [the localized reactions to] the stresses faced by rural communities under the rule of colonial regimes in the early twentieth century."[48] One of the largest uprisings to take place in the territory previously governed by the Qing, the Tapani Incident (Jiao ba nian shijian 噍吧哖事件), occurred two decades into Japanese rule, in 1915. In July of that year, two men, Yu Ching-fang 余清芳, a former bureaucrat and merchant, and Chiang

Ting 江定, a disgraced local district head, rallied an army of farmers and transient workers, drawn from nearby communities of Han settlers and Taivoan plains indigenous people, in a series of attacks on police stations in Tainan and Kaohsiung prefectures. The Tapani Incident was motivated by a mix of heady millenarian belief and economic discontent, especially against onerous taxes and the establishment of large-scale Japanese-owned sugar corporations that crowded out local producers and restricted the prices at which they could sell their crops. In retaliation, Japanese authorities arrested an estimated 1,957 people and sentenced 915 of them to death in summary court, sometimes extracting evidence by torture. 135 people were executed before the remainder of the sentences were converted to life terms.[49]

Japanese rule eventually brought the whole of Taiwan under centralized administration for the first time, a massive undertaking of mapping, policing and administration that strained the capacity of metropolitan Japan. But (like the ROC would a generation later) it also created different legal and conceptual regimes for administering the indigenous peoples of the newly conquered east versus the Han "islanders" and plains indigenous in the west. Paul D. Barclay describes this arrangement as sort of "weak legal pluralism" and a form of "bifurcated sovereignty."[50] In 1914, Japanese military and police forces captured Taroko Gorge (Tailuge xiagu 太魯閣峽谷)—the vast marble gorge carved out by the Liwu River (Liwu xi 立霧溪)—opening the surrounding mountains and the east coast to foreign rule in the name of colonial modernization. "After this year," Scott Simon explains, indigenous people in eastern Taiwan "endured the same measures taken in colonial situations worldwide: population transfers and the creation of traditional reserves, the transformation of traditional laws...and policies requiring new forms of capitalist productivity."[51] What the Japanese desired was the valuable bounty of the Central Mountains and East Rift Valley: camphor (a key ingredient in gunpowder), timber, tea, marble, and hydroelectric power, and the ability to name, pacify, supervise, marginalize, or enlist the people living there. In the mid-1930s, Japanese anthropologists fixed at nine the indigenous tribes of Taiwan:

the Amis, Atayal, Bunun, Paiwan, Puyuma, Rukai, Saisiyat, Tsou, and Yami (today more commonly called the Tao people, and who are native to Orchid Island), a classification that lasted until the turn of the twenty-first century.[52] That there are sixteen official tribes today is a testament to the relationship between democratization and the pursuit of indigenous rights, including name rectification of towns, mountains, and rivers, and finer-grained recognition of indigenous groupings based on differences in language, migration, kinship, cultural practice, political aspiration, and self-identification.

As Simon argues, the identities of two of the newly recognized peoples—the Truku and Seediq—were "crystalized" and "forged" in major confrontations with the Japanese that came to set them apart from the Atayal people they were both originally classified with.[53] The people who call themselves Truku fought the longest against the Japanese conquest of Taroko Gorge, outnumbered ten to one, utilizing the tricky, elevated terrain to their advantage to hold out for three months.[54]

Both the Japanese and the ROC regimes later designated Taroko Gorge as state land in the form of a national park. In 2019, the last year before the COVID-19 pandemic, it received an estimated 4.82 million visitors.[55] Only a fraction, however, venture on to the permit-only trails for serious hikers, which together trace the colonial history of the area. The Zhuilu Old Road (Zhuilu gudao 錐麓古道), where for a stretch hikers must walk in single file with their backs to the sheer rock, navigating by guidance ropes, was constructed in 1914 at the cost of the lives of thirty-seven indigenous workers.[56] The Dali-Datong Trail leads to two of the only indigenous villages in the area the Japanese permitted to remain at high altitude and did not forcibly relocate to the plains. Dali 大禮 and Datong 大同 are their names in Mandarin, which do not correspond in sound or definition to their names in the Truku language: Xoxos, meaning a "place with many snakes" and Skadang, meaning "molar teeth."[57]

The ancestors of the people now recognized as Seediq launched the last major uprising against Japanese rule in 1930. This incident that has been remembered both as an exemplar of indigenous resistance to colonialism and as the proximate cause of the devastation of the Seediq people and the loss of their traditional homelands. On October 27, the Seediq warrior Mona Rudao led men from six villages in coordinated attacks on police stations in Musha District (Wushe qu 霧社區), what is now Ren'ai District in Nantou County. With an arsenal of weapons they had amassed that morning, they descended upon Japanese spectators and schoolchildren gathered for a sports event at Musha Elementary School. In total, they killed 134 Japanese officers and civilians that day. In retaliation, authorities dispatched battalions of troops with artillery and dropped mustard gas bombs to dislodge the rebels from their positions in the mountains. Within two months, 644 Seediq had either been killed or committed ritual suicide, bringing the community nearly to the point of elimination.[58] At a February 24, 1931, meeting, members of the Taiwanese People's Party (Taiwan minzhong dang 台灣民眾黨), cofounded by the activist-physician Chiang Wei-shui 蔣渭水 as the first political party in the island's history, debated how to respond to the Government General's suppression of the Musha Rebellion.[59] The meeting was broken up by police, but the Taiwan People's Party reached out to the League of Nations to protest the use of chemical warfare against the Seediq.[60] As a strategy of colonial resistance, again prefiguring Taiwan's transnational political activism today, the People's Party sought to internationalize Taiwan's plight and to help Taiwan find a place of its own in the world, not simply as a satellite of the metropole or as a resource to be used for Japan's imperial project.

The task of reckoning with the violence of Japanese colonization, especially in the first two decades of rule and again in the late 1930s to 1945, when Taiwanese people and resources were turned to serve the needs of the Imperial Army under Japanese right-wing militarism, has in many ways been shaded over by the enormity of events after the end of World War II under the KMT. Today, Taiwan is experimenting with new ways of understanding and articulating the impact of Japanese colonialism that shift the focus away from comparing the respective crimes of successive colonial regimes towards the development of a new sense of Taiwanese subjectivity and agency during the 1920s and 1930s.

This experimentation with managing multiple and contending historical narratives is visible in the politics of national commemorations. In 2021, as the People's Republic of China marked the one-hundredth anniversary of the founding of the Chinese Communist Party, Taiwan was commemorating a different centennial: the birth of two political movements for Taiwanese enlightenment and self-rule, the League for the Establishment of a Taiwan Parliament (1921–1934) and the Taiwanese Cultural Association (TCA, 1921–1927). These commemorations disrupt and challenge multiple timelines about Chinese history under which Taiwan is routinely subsumed.

In 2021, these anniversaries intersected with the 110th National Day of the ROC on October 10, which commemorates the Xinhai Revolution of 1911, the uprising in Wuhan that led to the collapse of the Qing empire and the founding of the Republic by Dr Sun Yat-sen. Since Tsai Ing-wen assumed office in 2016, her administration had approached October 10 as a hybrid celebration of both the ROC and Taiwan, often foregrounding the latter over the former. The logos for "Double Ten Day" have been denuded of the red-white-and-blue color combination of the ROC flag, while the English-language slogans chosen for 2017, 2018, 2019, 2020 and 2021 were, respectively, "Better Taiwan," "Taiwan Together," "Taiwan Forward," "Proud of Taiwan," and "Taiwan National Day."[61] In her annual address on October 10, 2021, Tsai briefly acknowledged that it was the 110th National Day of the ROC but focused almost entirely on the seventy-two years since the ROC government's relocation to Taiwan.[62] Afterwards, You Si-kun 游錫堃, the DPP speaker of the legislature, delivered a speech that drew a clear distinction between Taiwanese history and ROC and PRC history, outlining a teleology of Taiwan's own that led to the current democratic way of life. The number that mattered the most for him was not seventy-two, or 110, but one hundred: the century since Taiwanese students studying in Tokyo formed the League for the Establishment of a Taiwan Parliament and began petitioning the Imperial Diet for a popularly elected parliament in Taiwan. That same year, their colleagues at home established a cultural association for self-education and consciousness-raising. "Democracy," You proclaimed, "has been Taiwan's century-long pursuit. Democracy has been embedded in Taiwan's genes for a hundred years."[63]

Seven days later, on October 17, Tsai gathered with descendants of the founding members of the league and the Taiwan Cultural Association for a concert at the Sun Yat-sen Memorial Hall (Guofu jinian guan 國父紀念館) in the Zhongshan District of Taipei, a 30,000-square-meter events complex completed in 1972 to honor the "founding father" of the Republic of China.[64] A physician and political activist, Sun anchored his program of Chinese republicanism in the "Three Principles of the People" (*San min zhuyi* 三民主義): ethnic nationalism (*minzu zhuyi* 民族主義), democracy (*minquan zhuyi* 民權主義), and social welfare (*minsheng zhuyi* 民生主義). Ironically, under Sun's successor Chiang Kai-shek, the Republic he inspired flouted these principles for the first eighty-five years of its existence, suspending national elections first in China and then in Taiwan in the name of wartime exigency. Only decades after its flight to Taiwan did the ROC government begin living up to the democratic ideals outlined in its early to mid-twentieth-century constitutions, pushed to it not by Chinese patriots but by people who called themselves Taiwanese.

As the festivities on October 17 highlighted, the movement for self-governance in Taiwan was born decades before the island would become part of the ROC. The setting of Sun Yat-sen Memorial Hall made the iconography of the centennial celebration even more arresting. Projected onto the stage were the words "Taiwan is the Taiwan of Taiwanese people" (*Taiwan shi Taiwanren de Taiwan* 台灣是台灣人的台灣), the slogan and rallying cry of the magazine *Taiwan Youth* (*Taiwan qingnian* 台灣青年), started in 1920. Neither the league nor the cultural association survived internal dissension and crackdowns on leftists and anti-colonial activists in the 1930s, but today they are often credited with inaugurating a continuous and ongoing struggle for self-determination. As the historian Chen Tsui-lien 陳翠蓮 argues, "This attempt to achieve 'self-determination', from the Japanese era continuing into the post-war era, constitutes a hundred-year-long dream chased by the Taiwanese."[65]

Chen's elastic framework groups together disparate movements against changing targets (Imperial Japan, the KMT party-state, the PRC), on the principle that they all show a basic demand for self-governance, even as the meaning of "Taiwanese"—and who identifies themselves as such—has shifted considerably over time. In 2021, as Taiwan held off the COVID-19 pandemic and its public life continued nearly as normal, the national day commemorations around Taipei and other cities showed how these once-forbidden origin stories were being themselves institutionalized into a national story that repurposed commemorative days and sites away from the ROC and towards Taiwan.

One could wander into the official government bookstore in the Taipei building that houses the Central News Agency, once the KMT state media outlet, and peruse a display of new books examining the league, TCA, and anti-Japanese and early anti-ROC activism, histories that remain almost entirely obscure in Anglophone discourse about Taiwan. Then have lunch at the upscale Walkingbook Restaurant (Kiâⁿ chheh 行冊) in the historic Datong District of Taipei, built on the site of the former Da-An Hospital (Daan yiyuan 大安醫院) that was run by Chiang Wei-shui, who also cofounded the TCA. Afterwards, one could walk next door to a pop-up exhibit celebrating Chiang's life and legacy and then attend a newly commissioned opera in his honor at the National Concert Hall (Guojia yingyueting 國家音樂廳) titled "Jail, as my Hotel" (*Naxie tien, Jiang Wei-shui zai lao li*那些天，蔣渭水在牢裡), depicting the twelve times he was imprisoned for his writing and organizing before his untimely death at just forty years old from typhoid in 1931.[66] One could take in a special exhibition at the National Museum of Taiwan Literature in Tainan featuring photo-real animations of key figures of the TCA speaking in period-accurate Taiwanese Hokkien and reminiscing about their roles as writers, actors, and teachers in the 1920s and 1930s.[67] And visit the NMTH, newly opened that year after a lengthy renovation, where the engaging, interactive section of the permanent exhibit covering the 1920s and 1930s featured life-size dioramas of modish Taiwanese men and women participating in all a modernizing culture had to offer: new clothing styles, new leisure activities, and new political and intellectual associations. One could also tune in to a podcast by the former Minister of Culture Cheng Li-chun 鄭麗君 and historian Wu Rwei-ren 吳叡人 and listen to them trace a direct line between the league, TCA, and the continuing effort to build a democratic society unified and resilient enough to withstand even the most daunting of geopolitical challenges posed by the PRC.[68]

International media reports and international relations analyses often speak of Taiwanese identity as "increasing," which misleadingly implies that it is a new phenomenon affecting cross-strait relations. In June 2021, the annual Election Study Center poll at National Chengchi University in Taipei reported that 62.3% of people surveyed claimed a Taiwanese identity exclusively, with 31.7% describing themselves as both Chinese and Taiwanese (*dou shi zhongguoren yu Taiwanren* 都是中國人與台灣人), and 2.8% as Chinese only (roughly proportional to the percentage of people alive who were born and raised in China or emigrated from the PRC in more recent years).[69] In 2008, the percentages were 48.4, 43.1, and 4.0, respectively. In 1992, the first year the survey was conducted, only 17.6% of people identified themselves as Taiwanese, far exceeded by the 25.5% who identified themselves as Chinese, and the 46.4% who chose both. Yet while Taiwanese identity is modern, as the many activities commemorating the centenary of the League for the Establishment of a Taiwan Parliament showed, it is not new. Rather, a Taiwanese identity was already being articulated in the 1920s among intellectuals and professionals—doctors, merchants, teachers, artists, and philanthropists— whose experience of second-class treatment and forced assimilation under Japanese rule gave rise to both a sense of commonality amongst themselves, and of difference vis-à-vis a more privileged class of outsiders.

There were several distinctive features of this nascent Taiwanese identity. First, it was formed in the context of demands for equal treatment under Japanese law and a degree of self-rule within a larger empire, rather than for nationhood. A national identity, and its concomitant— modernity—were supposed to be properties of metropolitan residents. By contrast, people in Taiwan were cast by the colonial government as backwards subjects in need of tutelage and forbidden from engaging in any activity that could be interpreted as constituting a "national struggle." For these reasons, Evan Dawley argues, early Taiwaneseness was expressed mostly in (mono)ethnic and cultural terms, triangulating itself between Imperial Japanese and Republican Chinese nationalisms.[70] Chiang Wei-shui, who took inspiration from contemporaneous social developments across the Strait, such as the May Fourth Movement, composed a song for the opening ceremony of the TCA in October 1921. Visitors to the NMTH can listen to a recording of the song and read a copy of the lyrics written in Chiang's hand, describing the Taiwanese as "Han descended Japanese subjects who are charged with serving as a harmonious link between these brothers [China and Japan]."[71] In an essay titled "Naming the Taiwanese" (*Taiwanren de mingcheng* 台灣人的 名稱), Huang Cheng-tsung 黃呈聰, a prominent member of the League for the Establishment of a Taiwanese Parliament, argued that the term "islanders" (*bendaoren* 本島人 or *hontōjin*) was inadequate to describe settlers of Chinese ancestry living in Taiwan. "No one knows that it refers to Taiwanese specifically," he wrote. "We propose to call ourselves 'Taiwanese people', so that no matter where we are, the meaning is clear." (Yet he was content that the offensive term *turen* 土人 or *dojin*, literally "people of the soil," continue to be used for "unassimilated" indigenous tribes.[72])

Second, the emergent Taiwanese identity of the 1920s was, or aspired to be, both island-wide and international in its outlook. Taiwan was Imperial Japan's first colony, a site on which Japanese officials attempted to showcase their ability to govern in an enlightened and modernizing way.[73] To that end, they invested heavily in sanitation, infrastructure, and communication, thus creating new connections between people who lived in different cities and villages around the island. By 1908, it was possible to travel by train down the west coast of the island, from Keelung in the north to Takao (later renamed Kaohsiung) in the south in one day, compared to the several days the journey used to take before the completion of the Taiwan Trunk (Zong Guan Xian 縱貫線) railway line.[74] The government-sanctioned *Taiwan Daily News* (Taiwan ri ri xin bao, or Taiwan nichinichi shinpō 臺灣日日新報) became the first daily newspaper with a circulation across the island. The Japanese-language edition was established in 1898, while a Chinese-language insert was published between 1901 and 1905; and again between 1911 and 1937.[75] The civic organizers behind the TCA strove to achieve a similar level of outreach. Affiliates sprang up across the island: at least four in Taipei and four in Hsinchu prefectures in the north, six in Taichung prefecture in central Taiwan, and five in Tainan, and three in Kaohsiung prefectures in the south.[76] The TCA and its local branches also inspired and overlapped a range of other new and socially conscious organizations aimed at educating and uplifting women, young people, laborers, and farmers, such as physical fitness clubs; theater and movie screening troupes; reading groups that read aloud the news; and raucous debate clubs covering topics like public health, Chinese history, and European philosophy. Taiwanese identity and Taiwanese modernization were inextricably linked.

Education thus became a critical institutional setting for exploring Taiwanese identity in the colonial period. Access to secondary schools for Taiwanese students was limited under the Japanese system and the training at the post-secondary level was restricted to medicine and pedagogy. The wealthy landowner Lin Hsien-tang 林獻堂 took funds slated for his grandmother's eightieth birthday celebration and, with other philanthropists, founded a high school in Taichung in 1915 specifically to educate young Taiwanese. It still operates today as the Taichung First Senior High School.

Students sent by wealthy families to Tokyo for education also played a role in constructing Taiwanese identity in the metropole. [77] Approximately 2,400 Taiwanese were studying in Japan in 1922, a number that rose to about 7,000 twenty years later.[78] These students hailed from different parts of the island but lived together in dormitories where, segregated from their Japanese peers, they read and debated the ideas and events of the day, from communism and the Russian Revolution to liberalism, and the ideas of self-determination that circulated after World War I in statements like Woodrow Wilson's Fourteen Points. They sought out opportunities to write and collaborate with their Korean, Chinese, and Filipino peers, seeking common cause with fellow colonized people in East and Southeast Asia.[79] In 1920, students in Japan founded the New People's Society (Xin min hui 新民會) and the magazine *Taiwan Youth*. Its inaugural issue, printed in July of that year, declared: "Taiwan, which is a part of the earth, and islanders, who are part of mankind, should rush to catch up with the new era, to develop a spiritual and material culture, and contribute to the great effort of transforming the world."[80]

The New People's Society was a precursor to the League for the Establishment of a Taiwanese Parliament that Legislative speaker You Si-kun spoke of in his national day address, the most prominent of numerous organizations and activities in the 1920s and 1930s that together were concerned with making Taiwan modern. The league advocated for a local legislature with control over budgetary matters, whose members would be chosen by voters in Taiwan regardless of ethnicity, thereby giving the much more numerous Taiwanese an advantage over the Japanese colonists. In thirteen years, the New People's Society and the league submitted fifteen petitions to the Imperial Diet for self-government.[81] Delegations, numbering in the hundreds of people, traveled to Tokyo to advocate for the goals of the league in meetings with Diet members. At its height, the petitioning movement built significant political constituencies in both Taiwan and Japan despite the opposition of the Taiwan Government-General, which did not want to relinquish its legislative powers. League delegates attracted eager and enthusiastic crowds on summer lecture tours back home. In a 1972 survey, Edward I-Te Chen counted a total of 17,262 Taiwanese who affixed their signatures to at least one of the fifteen petitions; nearly all the signatories were professionals and local officials, but of all educational backgrounds, and those with secondary or university schooling far outnumbered by those with only elementary-level or no formal schooling at all. "[It] must be emphasized," Chen noted, "that for anyone to sign a petition would mean divulging his identity, thus exposing himself to possible police retaliation and harassment by Japanese residents."[82] In this brief decade and a half when Japan itself seemed potentially on the path to liberalism, the league also won the support of prominent Japanese academics and legislators who were willing to introduce the petitions on the floor of the Diet.

Third, the promotion of literacy in local languages also played a role in formulating this early identity. As the linguist Su Huang-lan argues, it was at this point that the Romanized writing system for Taiwanese Hokkien known Pèh-ōe-jī (POJ) 白話字, invented by Western missionaries in the 1860s, shifted from being a tool "to facilitate education and proselytism in the [minority] Christian community, to a marker of Taiwanese ethnic identity," changing "from a 'church' language to a 'Taiwanese' written language."[83] This was partly due to the promotion of literacy and education in the early 1920s. POJ educators experimented with translating western novels; producing "nativist literature" that expressed a love for the land and natural environment; and writing philosophical and pedagogical essays that explored what it meant to be Taiwanese or have a Taiwanese consciousness. A writing system based on the Roman alphabet had the potential to reach a greater number of people, but texts in Taiwanese written with Chinese characters flourished as well, particularly songs, poetry, and plays.

This embryonic movement to read and write in Taiwanese also reveals how successive governments targeted the systems and institutions through which Taiwanese identity could be expressed. In the authoritarian period after 1945, Taiwanese language was systematically marginalized by the ROC government, which restricted the production and circulation of POJ literature in the name of Mandarinzation. By comparison, Japanese officials and educators in the colonial state had displayed a greater willingness to learn Taiwanese and even POJ to communicate with their colonized subjects, even if in principle such usage was only meant as a stopgap until all people in Taiwan achieved Japanese fluency. KMT policy also deliberately targeted the use of spoken Taiwanese. Beginning in 1956 until 1987, students and teachers were forbidden from speaking Taiwanese and other non-Mandarin Sinitic languages like Hakka and all indigenous languages in schools; children were beaten, humiliated, fined, and made to wear dunce caps for transgressions.[84] In 1982, the amended Broadcast and Television Act (Guangbo dianshi fa 廣播電視法) mandated that programming be based primarily in Mandarin and use of so-called dialects (*fangyan* 方言) be reduced year on year.[85]

Today, according to the 2020 Census by the Executive Yuan, while 65.9% of respondents born before 1955 speak Taiwanese as their primary language, only 11% of those born between 1996 and 2005 do, and 7.4% of those born between 2006 and 2014. The corresponding percentages for Mandarin are 28.5%, 88.5%, and 92.1%.[86] These statistics are even more astonishing since Mandarin was a foreign language in Taiwan prior to 1945 and the arrival of new Chinese settlers. "Mother languages" (*muyü* 母語)—such as Taiwanese, Hakka, and indigenous languages like Atayal, Amis, and Paiwan—have been offered as second-language classes in some elementary schools a few hours a week since the early 1990s and more broadly since the early 2000s. These classes were expanded to the secondary level starting in 2022.[87]

In these classes, Taiwanese is taught using up to three different orthographies: romanization system adapted from POJ; a transliteration system derived from Bopomofo (*zhuyin fuhao* 注音符號), originally designed for Mandarin use; and Han Chinese characters (*hanzi* 漢字). Yet even as a younger generation is gaining limited exposure to Taiwanese-language writing systems that their Taiwanese-speaking parents and grandparents were denied, they are much less likely to have opportunities to use the language with their friends, colleagues, or even their families. Primary and secondary schools in Taiwan, public or private, no longer punish students for speaking Taiwanese but still teach subject matter material almost exclusively in Mandarin. Occasional controversies, such as the time a mathematics professor at National Taiwan University (NTU) began teaching his subject in Taiwanese in 1996, only served to highlight the normalization of Mandarin and the marginalization of Taiwanese since the Japanese period.[88] As Taiwanese identity rises and is freer to claim than at any point in the past one hundred years, the language that this identity was first expressed in is endangered and threatened with extinction within another generation.

THREE: LIVING IN REVOLUTIONARY TIME

Taiwan has multiple overlapping histories that shape how Taiwanese identify themselves and make meaning of their lives. Outside Taiwan, however, these pre-1949 histories are rarely acknowledged when discussing what sort of place Taiwan is and who its people are. The norm of starting the Taiwan story in 1949 with a "divided China" leaves out entirely the Japanese colonial era and the nascent Taiwanese and indigenous identities produced through discrimination and forced acculturation. It also misses by just two years the February 28 Incident in 1947, one of the most important reasons why even four decades of Sinicization under the ROC failed to extinguish the hope for a democratic nation governed by people who saw themselves as Taiwanese and not displaced Chinese.

The unification of Taiwan and China is often normalized as an inevitable, if deferred, future by both Beijing and the realists working in foreign policy and international relations. On January 1, 1979, the day the United States formally established relations with the PRC, the National People's Congress delivered a "Message to Taiwan Compatriots," announcing that their goal was no longer to "liberate" the island from the KMT using military force, but to "peacefully reunify" with it.[89]

Forty years later, Xi Jinping reiterated in his own New Year's address that "reunification" was "the great trend of history" and that it was the responsibility of everyone in Taiwan and China to work together towards the full glory of a restored Chinese nation. He pledged that "the social system and lifestyles of Taiwan compatriots will be fully respected" and their "private property, religious beliefs, and legitimate rights and interests...fully guaranteed." Nowhere in this speech was to be found a promise that a future Taiwan Province could keep the democratic governance they currently enjoyed, even at a provincial or sub-provincial level. Although he set no timeline, Xi stated that the Taiwan problem "should not be passed down generation after generation" and reserved for the PRC "the option to take any necessary measures" to block what he called the "interference of external forces and [the] extremely small number of 'Taiwan independence' separatists and their separatist activities."[90]

If unification with the PRC is indeed in Taiwan's future, it would be a tectonic disruption to global geopolitics. Thinking of unification only as a potential outcome, however, misses that it already happened once before: from 1945 to 1949, when the KMT began occupying Taiwan by agreement of the Allied powers while it still maintained a tenuous hold on the government in China. It was at this moment when the short history of the ROC began intersecting with the much longer history of Taiwan. In the Cairo Declaration of November 27, 1943, the "Three Great Allies" (the United States, the United Kingdom, and the Republic of China) stipulated that "all the territories Japan has stolen from the Chinese, such as Manchuria, Formosa [Taiwan], and the Pescadores [Penghu] shall be restored to the Republic of China." In essence, they argued that the ROC was the legitimate inheritor of Qing-era land, leaving out the fact that the Qing had not governed the entirety of the island.[91] The Potsdam Declaration of July 26, 1945, also stripped Japan of sovereignty over Taiwan. Between the end of 1945 and 1947, an estimated 350,000 to 390,000 Japanese were repatriated, while Taiwanese wives of Japanese men, along with their children, were given the option to leave as well.[92] Chen Yi 陳儀, a former governor of Fujian Province whom Chiang Kai-shek appointed the new Chief Executive of Taiwan, traveled to the island under American escort and accepted the Japanese instrument of surrender on October 25. He proclaimed it "Retrocession Day" (Guangfujie 光復節). The label connoted a family reunion, a rejoining of territories based on bloodlines. The same analogies are used to argue for a "reunification" of Taiwan and the People's Republic today.

Then, from February to May of 1947, less than eighteen months after the start of unification, troops dispatched by Chiang Kai-shek would slaughter an estimated 20,000 Taiwanese, including students, lawyers, doctors, artists, businessmen, and community leaders, both openly on the streets and in closed-door executions, after summary judgment or no judgment at all. Explaining why this happened is inexplicable using the terminology and frameworks under which KMT rule was established in the first place.

The conflict between those who were described by the KMT as *benshengren* 本省人 (Chinese descendants who had already been living in Taiwan prior to "retrocession" and were "from the province") and *waishengren* 外省人 (soldiers, administrators, bureaucrats, and businessmen who began arriving from "outside the province" in late 1945)—is often explained in terms of mutual disillusionment between people who had been conditioned see each other as similar in nature. For *waishengren* who had fought in the Second Sino-Japanese War from 1937 to 1945 and been occupied and displaced by the Japanese Imperial Army, it could seem like a shock and betrayal to meet ostensibly Chinese people who spoke Japanese, bore Japanese names, and were proud of the improvements in their quality of life during the first half of the twentieth century. On average, Taiwanese enjoyed a higher standard of living than their counterparts in China did. Yet as the historian Dominic Meng-hsuan Yang writes, the "earlier dislocation and suffering [of *waishengren*] at the hands of the Japanese strengthened their bias against the semi-Japanese *benshengren*," convincing them that the "poor locals needed to be coached, educated, and re-Sinicized before being treated as equals"[93].

Contained within the attitudes of first-generation *waishengren* were questions that are still lie at the center of every debate about Taiwan and its future today: who the people living there *really* are, and whether it is possible for them to adopt new identities over time as a result of education, changes in government, and encounters with "the other", or if they are somehow essentially and always Chinese.

Initial optimism in Taiwan at the end of Japanese rule and union with a Chinese republic quickly evaporated. This was due not only to disidentification between *waishengren* and *benshengren* but also the ways in which ROC rule came to echo the Japanese regime before it, in terms of the power relations between new settlers and the preexisting population and the drainage of money and natural resources to serve the war making needs of the mother country. Evan Dawley contends that "Early governance by the Nationalists was, in essence, a recolonization of Taiwan..."[94] The new Taiwan Provincial Administrative Office (Taiwansheng xingzheng zhangguan gongshu 台灣省行政長官公署), overwhelmingly staffed by *waishengren*, was endowed with combination of legislative, executive, and judicial powers similar to those of the Japanese Government-General. This raised, once again, the colonial-era issue of self-rule, or the lack thereof, within a larger metropolitan state. According to historian Steven Phillips, "Only three of the first twenty-three county magistrates' posts or mayorships, and one of the twenty-one highest posts in the provincial government, were delegated to Taiwanese. Islanders made up only a small portion of mid-level officials in the various departments."[95]

In short order, Japanese-era corporations and state-run enterprises were reconstituted as KMT-controlled entities, such as the Taiwan Sugar Corporation (formed by combining the assets of four Japanese sugar companies), Taiwan Power Company, and Taiwan Provincial Monopoly Bureau (formerly the Monopoly Bureau of the Taiwan Governor's Office, which controlled the production and sale of tobacco and alcohol products).[96] The new government also claimed private property held by the departing Japanese, giving newly arrived *waishengren* a pretext to take advantage of and evict Taiwanese who had attempted to purchase it.[97] Precipitously integrated into a Chinese economy ravaged by civil war, Taiwan began to suffer some of the same problems plaguing the mainland: hyperinflation, unemployment, hoarding, speculation, profiteering, and a scarcity of essential goods. The dissident lawyer Peng Ming-min 彭明敏, who would go on to represent the Democratic Progressive Party in the first direct presidential election in 1996, was a young student at the time of the handover. In his memoir *A Taste of Freedom*, he accused Chiang Kai-shek's "representatives on Formosa [of] extending to our island the abuses that weakened his position throughout China and brought about his ultimate downfall. By the end of 1946, [they] were acting with unlimited and desperate greed."[98]

A minor incident became the launching point for a wider movement for local representation and autonomy that was soon ruthlessly repressed. On February 27, 1947, officers from the Taiwan Provincial Monopoly Bureau tried to confiscate contraband from a widowed woman selling cigarettes outside the Tianma Tea House in what is now the Datong District in Taipei. When she resisted, a crowd of locals rushed to intercede. In the ensuing melee, an officer shot and killed a bystander. The next day, protestors marched down the streets of Taipei carrying gongs and calling for a general strike. A group of *benshengren* Taiwanese occupied the government's radio headquarters and urged their listeners to march on the Provincial Administrative Office. The governor's guards opened fire on the unarmed men who appeared at the gates. Pent-up frustration from the preceding eighteen months was released in days of parades and riots across the island against KMT officials. The violence also affected *waishengren* civilians, who were attacked in their shops or homes or on the streets for their inability to speak Japanese or Taiwanese.[99]

On March 2, leading Taipei citizens established a 228 Incident Settlement Committee (Er er ba shijian chuli weiyuanhui 二二八事件處理委員會), both to restore order and to put forth political demands to the new ROC government, including a separate constitution for Taiwan and the popular election of mayors and magistrates. Parallel settlement committees sprang up in Keelung, Yilan, and Banqiao in the north, Taichung in the center, Hualien in the east, and Tainan and Kaohsiung in the south.[100] As they had under Japanese rule, the local elite positioned themselves as the legitimate representatives of the Taiwanese people, while disclaiming pretensions to independence or separatism. In the list of thirty-two demands they issued on March 6, the Taipei Settlement Committee stated, "We are all sons of the Yellow Emperor and all of the Han race. The quality of national governance depends on all citizens of the Republic."[101] Often overlooked are the roles played by indigenous leaders in this tense transitory period, such as the teacher, poet, and politician Uyonge Yatauyungana, who led a group of his fellow Tsou Taiwanese on a failed attempt to secure the airport in the southern city of Chiayi. Yatauyungana, an advocate of Tsou autonomy, was executed on April 17, 1954, on trumped-up charges of spying.[102]

For his part, Chen Yi stalled for time while secretly wiring the mainland for reinforcements. On March 8, a contingent of soldiers arrived at the northern port city of Keelung and another at Kaohsiung in the south, the same day that General Chang Mu-tao 張慕陶, Commander of the Fourth Gendarme Regiment, gave his word to the Taipei Settlement Committee that "the central government will not dispatch troops to Taiwan...I can risk my life to guarantee that the central government will not take any military action against Taiwan. I speak these words out of sincere attachment to this Province and to the nation."[103] The untruth of his words was tragically clear by nightfall. Organizers of the various settlement committees were systematically identified, rounded up, and killed. For the next three weeks, the soldiers were given free rein to engage in torture, rape, robbery, and extra-judicial executions by indiscriminate open fire, bayonetting, mutilation, beheading, and drowning. No part of the island was spared.

For decades, discussion or even acknowledgment of the KMT's crimes during the February 28 Incident was forbidden in Taiwan and punishable by arrest or imprisonment. It was an act of historical erasure that shaped the lives of generations of Taiwanese people. Yet in the two weeks after the widow was accosted outside the Tianma Tea House, independent local newspapers churned out reports of the escalating tensions and the arrival of Chinese troops. According to historian Yen-kuang Kuo, the reports focused on two trends: "the spontaneous, unorganized, and violent responses of the Taiwanese masses towards the KMT authorities' high-handed policies, on the one hand, and the local elite leaders' peaceful and politicized negotiations with the authorities, on the other."[104] By mid-March, however, the regime had shut down most of the independent press, with only KMT-controlled or affiliated outlets permitted to publish. The regime blamed the unrest on subversive elements, characterizing the settlement committees as pro-Communist and pro-Japanese, while simultaneously downplaying or failing to mention the killings committed by ROC troops.[105]

Foreign reporters proved harder to silence, however. Stories about the February 28 Incident and the massacres that followed appeared in major American newspapers and magazines such as the *San Francisco Chronicle*, *Los Angeles Times*, *Washington Post*, and *The Nation*, pinning the Taiwanese civilian death toll at 5,000 to 10,000 and detailing both the systematic targeting of the Taiwanese elite and the atrocities carried out at the hands of the regime's soldiers.[106] A report by the *New York Times* on March 29, 1947, by the Nanjing-based correspondent Tillman Durdin, summarized eyewitness accounts by foreigners who had just returned to China from Taiwan. An American testified that "for a time everyone seen on the streets [in Taipei] was shot at, homes were broken into, and occupants killed. In the poorer sections the streets were said to have been littered with dead..." Two women whose nationalities were not specified told Durdin that in the southern city of Pingtung "The people were machine-gunned...The man who had served as the town's spokesman was killed. His body was left for a day in a park, and no one was permitted to remove it." A Briton recounted that in Kaohsiung, "where unarmed Formosans had taken over the running of the city...Chinese soldiers from an outlying fort deployed through the streets killing hundreds with machine-guns and rifles and raping and looting. Formosan leaders were thrown into prison, many bound with thin wire that cut deep into the flesh."[107] Responding to the internationalization of the crisis, Taiwanese activists called for intervention by the United Nations or the establishment of an American protectorate on the island, harkening back to the cries for international aid and assistance after the signing of the Treaty of Shimonoseki in 1895 and the Musha Incident in 1930.[108]

By the end of 1947, Taiwanese independence was being defined as a political aspiration, building on the activism of the Japanese colonial period and seeking to mobilize the institutions and ideas of a new international system emerging after World War II. Joshua Liao, a leading figure of the movement, submitted a petition to the new United Nations in 1948 calling for Taiwanese self-determination, later published under the title *Formosa Speaks*, one of numerous manifestos, articles, and magazines calling for international support.[109]

In Taiwan, however, the KMT party-state began enforcing the forgetting or outright denial of the February 28 Incident. Abroad, the memory of the uprising was eroded by the relentlessness of the news cycle and the support that the United States provided to the successive Chiang dictatorships, as the leaders of "Free China" during the Cold War. Today, the statements that "Taiwan and China split in 1949" or that "Taiwan and China have been governed separately since 1949" often appear in Anglophone analysis as a shorthand explainer for why there is tension in the Taiwan Strait, focusing the reader's attention on the moment of disjunction rather than the brevity and terror of the union preceding it. The result is a public discourse in the West that often looks towards unification of Taiwan and China a resolution rather than an accelerant of one of the major geopolitical difficulties in East Asia today. Without awareness of this history, unification can never bring epistemic closure, but only mortal danger for the Taiwanese and the beginnings of yet another drive for self-governance, the same drive that keeps the "Taiwan question" alive and open now.

Within Taiwan today, this history is clear. Democracy has allowed it to be written into the fabric of society and into the subjectivity of Taiwanese people. At the NMTH, the section on February 28 begins with the heading "Striding Towards Democracy," (*Zou xiang min zhu zhe tiao lu* 走向民主這條路) pinpointing the uprising as the start of a harrowing process of pushing for self-governance that culminated in the unlikely democratization of the Republic of China government.[110] Their embrace of a democratic way of life, in turn, is the primary reason that Taiwanese reject political union with the PRC, and one of the primary means— alongside their key role in powering the twenty-first century digital economy—through which they have mobilized international support in a post–Cold War world increasingly divided along democratic and authoritarian lines.

Yet there remains a deep refusal in the international system and its structures of power to see Taiwan as a country or as worthy of nationhood. One explanation is that it has not followed a particular postcolonial national blueprint: armed rebellion, prolonged war, total defeat of the previous government, and the declaration of a new nation. According to this line of thinking, Taiwan—still governed as part of the rump Republic of China and wanting recognition without sacrifice—has been rightly denied the benefits of being called a nation.

This notion imagines nationhood as forged from a singular moment of revolutionary crises and awakening. The uprisings against the corruption of the KMT that began on February 28, 1947, however, marked the start of a decades-long campaign for Taiwanese self-rule that has thus far defeated two projects aimed at cross-Strait unification, one by the ROC and the other the PRC. Taiwan's post–World War II trajectory is thus explicable as an instantiation of revolutionary time, in which the possibility of "breaking open the historical continuum" (in the words of political theorist Kimberly Hutchings) and disrupting seemingly foreordained outcomes is ever-present.[111] If we take revolutions to be interruptive processes that create space for seemingly unlikely futures, then since February 28, 1947, Taiwan has been living in revolutionary time, a horizon with an unknown ending date.

FOUR: XINJIANG, TIBET, AND HONG KONG TODAY, TAIWAN TOMORROW?

The 1949 framework comes packaged with its own resolution, namely, unification and absorption into the PRC along the lines of Hong Kong, Tibet, and Xinjiang. When Chinese officials and Western policy observers alike pronounce that unification is inevitable and desirable, they are acting to deny Taiwan and Taiwanese the right to an open-ended future. As late as September 2018, American foreign policy commentator Peter Beinart proposed in *The Atlantic* that "if China renounces the use of force, the United States should support its reunification with Taiwan along the principle of 'one country, two systems'. The US should ask China to commit publicly not to station troops or Communist Party officials in Taiwan, and to let Taiwan manage its domestic political affairs." He continued: "Would Beijing adhere to such an agreement once unification occurred? The best precedent is Hong Kong."[112] In January 2019, political scientist Zhiqun Zhu claimed in the *Washington Post* that Xi Jinping's New Years' speech showed that he was open to "inject[ing] a level of self-determination for Taiwan into the unification model" and that if only Taiwan would compromise, it would see that it could "use its vibrant democracy as a tool to shape the future of the Chinese mainland. Beijing says anything can be discussed under 'one China.' Taiwan certainly can and should raise its preconditions for unification."[113] The column ran with a photo of Tsai Ing-wen and this caption: "Taiwan's leader said that the people of the island want to maintain self-rule despite recent electoral gains [in the November 2018 midterm elections] by the Beijing-friendly opposition party [the KMT]." Whether the KMT would indeed be content with running only in provincial-level elections in a future 'one China' is unknown, and deliberately left ambiguous by the party's own leadership.

Both the Beinart and Zhu pieces appeared just months before the start of the 2019 protests in Hong Kong, in the wake of which a wide range of civil liberties—such as freedom of speech and the press— rapidly collapsed, followed by the exile or imprisonment of thousands of politicians, journalists, academics, students, and protesters, including the very young and obscure. Yet in 2014 Hong Kong had already gone through the Umbrella Movement, the name given to the mass occupations calling without success for universal suffrage and direct election of the city's chief executive.[114] Then in 2017, reports began circulating about the mass detention of Uyghur Muslims in "reeducation" camps in Xinjiang in the far west of the People's Republic, in response to bouts of inter- ethnic violence between Uyghurs and Han Chinese. With more than an estimated one million Uyghurs locked away in the camps, this is the largest-scale internment of an ethnic and religious group since the Holocaust in the mid-twentieth century.[115]

Near the end of the 2019 mass protests in Hong Kong, on December 8, a small group of participants who disguised their identities by wearing masks painted with the light turquoise flag of East Turkestan (the preferred name of Xinjiang for those who support an independent Uyghur nation) carried banners reading: "Yesterday's Uyghur and Tibet, Today's Hong Kong, Tomorrow's Taiwan" (*Zuori jiangzang, jinri xianggang, minri Taiwan* 昨日疆藏，今日香港，明日台灣).[116] This, of course, is a mimesis of the narrative that the CCP under Xi Jinping hopes will play out, a resolution of what it considers to be an open wound from the Qing era and achievement of what he calls "the Great Rejuvenation of the Chinese nation." The Taiwanese, by contrast, see the same teleology as a warning. A goal of Taiwanese nationalism is to ensure that the time between "today" and "tomorrow" will be indefinite, expressing the hope that Taiwan will be able to take a different path than Xinjiang, Tibet, or Hong Kong. The December march was sponsored by the Civil

Human Rights Front, a coalition made up of some of the most prominent pro-democracy organizations in Hong Kong. It was disbanded after a National Security Law was passed in June 2020. Some activists brought this warning across the Strait. On January 10, 2020, a group of black-clad Hong Kongers stood outside an election eve rally for Tsai Ing-wen holding a small yellow poster that read "Yesterday February 28, Today Hong Kong," alerting young Taiwanese to their experience of living under a unified China. The sign created a doubled timeline that compared Taiwan's unification with China under the KMT party-state to Hong Kong's situation today under the CCP.[117]

A visitor to the NMTH, however, would not necessarily be aware of the narratives that tie Taiwan's future to that of Hong Kong, Tibet, and Xinjiang, and therefore to the PRC. For all its focus on the regional and global political forces that have shaped Taiwan's history, indigenous, Japanese-era, and Republican alike, the museum ends its permanent exhibit with no commentary at all on the threat that Taiwanese people face from the PRC today, and how that threat works in part by denying that Taiwan has a history of its own.

Instead, the visit concludes with sections on building a more multicultural and inclusive Taiwanese society, and domestic challenges that stem from Taiwan's key position in global supply chains, ranging from migrant worker abuses to weak labor unions to environmental degradation.[118] In doing so, it conjures a fantasy in which the Taiwanese are tasked only with confronting the legacy of settler colonialism starting from the seventeenth century and the authoritarianism and hypergrowth of the second half of the twentieth century—and are free to do so without having their time, attention, and resources occupied by the possibility of another Chinese military takeover. As such, the exhibit ends not with a fully contextualized contemporaneous history but with imagination— not with a Taiwan headed inexorably towards absorption by a Chinese superpower but a Taiwan that stands on its own. This is a form of denial, reflecting frequent criticisms by those in the Western policy-making space that Taiwan has not done enough to ensure its own preparedness and defense. This is also a form of defiance: a determination to write, for however long it is possible, a story that sees Taiwan—not China—as the rightful endpoint.

Notes

1. "Architectural Features," National Museum of Taiwan History website.
2. "Taiwan history museum to open in Tainan City," *Taiwan Today.*
3. Permanent Exhibition, placard titled "Meiyou qiangquan kongzhi de yizuo ziyou dao" 沒有強權控制的一座自由島 [A free island uncontrolled by any regime], National Museum of Taiwan History, Tainan.
4. Yang and Chang, "Understanding the Nuances of Waishengren," 110.
5. Andrade, *How Taiwan Became Chinese,* 19.
6. Andrade, 9.
7. See the excellent, detailed discussions in Chiu, *The Colonial 'Civilizing' Process,* 33–48 (quote is from page 43) and Clulow, "The Art of Claiming," 20–24.
8. Andrade, *How Taiwan Became Chinese,* 2.
9. Jacobs, "Whither Taiwanization?" 571.
10. Permanent Exhibition, placard titled "Shanhai zhi jian de gongcun yu jingzhu 山海之間的共存與競逐 [Coexistence and competition amid mountains and oceans], National Museum of Taiwan History, Tainan.
11. Teng, *Taiwan's Imagined Geography,* 3. Teng writes, "The annexation of Taiwan was only one incident in the much larger phenomenon of Qing expansionism, a phenomenon that scholars have recently begun to treat as an example of imperialism, comparable to European imperialisms. Following the conquest of China proper, the Manchu rulers of the Qing dynasty pursued numerous campaigns on China's frontiers."
12. Shepherd, *Statecraft and Political Economy,* 161 (based on a Japanese census of 1905).
13. Millward, "We need a new approach to teaching modern Chinese history." Millward's essay began as a review and critique of Klaus Mühlhahn's book *Making China Modern: From the Great Qing to Xi Jinping* (Cambridge, MA: Harvard University Press, 2019).
14. Hale, "'Always campaign time.'"
15. "Amendments to the Constitution of the Republic of China.".
16. Mona, "Conceptualizing Indigenous Historical Justice Toward a Mutual Reconciliation with State in Taiwan."
17. Simon, *Truly Human,* 43.
18. Simon, 43.
19. Simon, "Negotiating Power," 731.

20. Cheung, "Taiwan in Time," 8.
21. Uradyn Bulag, "Nationality 民族,", 151; and Brady, "Unifying the Ancestral Land," 797.
22. Tsai, "President Tsai Apologizes Indigenous Peoples on Behalf of Government."
23. Rudd, "2008: National Apology to the Stolen Generations"; and Harper, "Statement of apology to former students of Indian Residential Schools."
24. Munsterhjelm, *Living Dead in the Pacific*.
25. Sia, "Crafting Aboriginal Nations in Taiwan."
26. Simon, "Taiwan's Indigenized Constitution," 3, 8.
27. "New Partnership Between the Government of Taiwan and Aboriginal Nations" signed September 10, 1999, partially reprinted online in the concluding remarks of the virtual exhibit "Map for Getting to Know the Tribes" by the Digital Museum of Taiwan Indigenous People. In Mandarin, the first three of seven pledges items are: "1) chengren taiwan yuanzhuminzu ziran zhuquan 承認台灣原住民族之自然主權; 2) tuidong yuanzhuminzu zizhi 推動原住民族自治; and 3) yu Taiwan yuanzhuminzu dijie tudi tiaoyue與台灣原住民族締結土地條約." For further discussion of the "New Partnership," see Mona, "International Perspective on the Constitutionality of Indigenous People's Rights," and Hung, "A Postcolonial Perspective on the State's Registration of Traditional Cultural Expressions," 218–220.
28. Chen, "A State within a State." The Mandarin original reads: 「接著於2002年10月正式以總統的身分，透過原住民各族傳統的締約儀式，代表政府與原住民族完成『新夥伴關係協定』的再肯認，明確的宣示原住民族是台灣這塊土地最早的主人，原住民族所擁有的自然主權是優先於國家而存在。」
29. Chen, "A State within a State," 104. The Mandarin original reads: 「還依稀記得於2004年總統大選電視辯論會時，本人曾說過，『希望在未來催生新憲法的過程中能夠把台灣政府於原住民族的新夥伴關係，也就是郭總有國的準國與國關係，在新憲法中有原住民專章明列。』」
30. "The Indigenous Peoples Basic Law," amended June 20, 2018, Laws and Regulations Database of the ROC (Taiwan), Ministry of Justice.
31. Liu, "Taitung councilors oppose recognition of the Siraya"; and Wu, "First argument at court of the Siraya constitutional interpretation case."
32. Hsieh, "Restoring Pingpu Indigenous Status and Rights," 239.

33. Wu, Chiu, and Chung "Aboriginal Land Boundary Draft Rules Meet Criticism," 3; and Fang, "'Why do indigenous Taiwanese have to agree to [use of] private land?'"
34. Gerber, "Protesters decry Aboriginal land policy proposal," 3.
35. Hioe, "Indigenous Occupation in 228 Memorial Park Dismantled."
36. Lin, "On 228, I choose to stand with Taiwan's Indigenous Peoples."
37. For more on Tibet and Xinjiang in the early twenty-first century, see recent books including Lixiong Wang and Tsering Shakya, *The Struggle for Tibet* (New York: Verso, 2009) and Darren Byler, *Terror Capitalism* (Durham, NC: Duke University Press, 2021).
38. See earlier discussion of Xi Jinping's New Year's Day speech 2019, chapter 1, p. 26-27 [but below you say that I should not refer to page numbers? The original "23" referenced what was p. 23 of the manuscript, now p. 26-27.]
39. Indigenous Historical Justice and Transitional Justice Committee, "Indigenous Peoples of Taiwan to President Xi Jinping of China."
40. Kuo, "From the Rover Incident to the Nanjia Treaty – Whose Conflict? Whose Treaty?"
41. Indigenous Historical Justice and Transitional Justice Committee, "Indigenous Peoples of Taiwan to President Xi Jinping of China.".
42. For detailed coverage of the short-lived history of the Republic of Formosa, see Alsford, *Transitions to Modernity in Taiwan*, from where the quotations in this paragraph are taken.
43. Cited in Alsford, *Transitions to Modernity*, 42.
44. Alsford, 156.
45. Davidson, *The Island of Formosa, Past and Present*, 279.
46. Alsford, *Transitions to Modernity*, 157.
47. Davidson, *The Island of Formosa*, 280-282.
48. Katz, "Governmentality and its Consequences in Colonial Taiwan," 390.
49. Katz, 388–389.
50. Barclay, *Empire of Outcasts*, 17.
51. Simon, "Making Natives," 79.
52. Sun, "Indigenous Voices: The Cry of Taiwan's Aboriginal Peoples."
53. Simon, "Making Natives," 85, 91.
54. Simon, 84–85.
55. Ministry of the Interior, "'Mountain Moon Bridge' Overcomes the Dangerous Obstacles of the Canyon and Wins the Public Construction Golden Quality Award."
56. Xie, "Taroko Gorge from Multiple Angles.".

57. National Museum of Taiwan History, "Skadang: [The] Place Where Molar Teeth Were Found," in "Place Names Tell Stories.".

58. Berry, *The Musha Incident*, 1–2.

59. The Taiwan People's Party of the Japanese era is not the same party as the TPP founded by Ko Wen-je in 2019.

60. Kerr, *Formosa*, 145–146; and Cheung, "Taiwan in Time: Fractured Resistance," 8.

61. Cheng, Liu, Chiu, and Lee, "National flag and name are not seen in the visuals for National Day, suspected of [promoting] independence in English."

62. Tsai, "President Tsai delivers 2021 National Day Address."

63. Liu, "Double Ten Day Ceremony Speaker You Si-kun."

64. Yeh, "Commemorating the centennial of the Cultural Association."

65. Chen, "Taiwan belongs to the Taiwanese."

66. Chiang Wei-shui's Cultural Foundation, "Cantata: Jail as My Hotel."

67. National Museum of Taiwan Literature "The Abiding Light of a Century-old Beacon" and "Centennial of the Cultural Association, National Taiwan Literature Museum's "'100 years of love letters special exhibition', Using love letters handed down to convey passion in a ruthless world."

68. Cheng and Wu, "Liberty and Government – To become a free person, Imagining our Community," 02:42.

69. See earlier discussion of this survey data in chapter 1.

70. Dawley, *Becoming Taiwanese*, 20–21.

71. Chiang, "Taiwan Cultural Association Song."

72. Chen, "Taiwan belongs to the Taiwanese."

73. Nadine Heé notes that in the "historiography on Japanese colonialism, there is a predominant tendency to describe Korea as the colony where the population revolted against Japanese policies and violent conflicts were regular occurrences. Taiwan, by contrast, is usually portrayed as a 'model colony' – a successful modernization project of so-called 'scientific colonialism'…" in "Taiwan under Japanese Rule," 632.

74. Taylor, "Colonial Takao," 59.

75. Liao, "Print Culture and the Emergent Public Sphere in Colonial Taiwan, 1895–1945," 84. A full Chinese-language insert was produced between 1905 and 1911.

76. Permanent exhibition placard titled "Taiwan wenhua xiehui zuzhi fazhan fenbu tu" 台灣文化協會組織發展分布圖 [Map of the Taiwan Cultural Association's Organizational Development] at Taiwan Xin

Wenhua Yundong Jinian Guan 台灣新文化運動紀念館 [Taiwan New Cultural Movement Memorial Museum] in Taipei.

77. A classic study of education in the Japanese era is Tsurumi, *Japanese Colonial Education in Taiwan, 1895–1945*.

78. Barclay, "Japanese Empire in Taiwan.".

79. Chapters 2 through 4 of Chen Tsui-lien's *The Dream of Self-Governance* have been extremely helpful.

80. Chen, "Taiwan belongs to the Taiwanese.".

81. Chen, "Formosan Political Movements Under Japanese Colonial Rule, 1914–1937," 483.

82. Chen, 484–485.

83. Su, "Writing 'Taiwanese,'" 110, 112.

84. Wu, "Language Planning and Policy in Taiwan"; and Sandel, "Linguistic Capital in Taiwan," 530. During the Kōminka period (1936–1945), authorities also prohibited public education in languages other than Japanese.

85. "Articles of the Broadcast and Television Act no longer in effect." The now-defunct Article 20 reads: 「電台對國內廣播播音語言應以國語為主，方言應逐年減少」.?

86. National Statistics Office, 2020 Population and Housing Census.

87. "Editorial: 'Bentu' Education Cannot Wait," 8.

88. Xu Tianren, "Don't let your mother tongue be lost to memory [beirang muyu xiaoshi de jiyi]," *China Times*, November 8, 1997, 11.

89. Metzler, *Taiwan's Transformation*, 69.

90. Xi, "Working Together to Realize Rejuvenation of the Chinese Nation.".

91. "The Cairo Declaration," 448–449.

92. Dawley, *Becoming Taiwanese*, 252.

93. Yang, *The Great Exodus from China*, 114.

94. Dawley, *Becoming Taiwanese*, 249.

95. Phillips, *Between Assimilation and Independence*, 70.

96. Kollar, "Cultivating (post)colonialism," 244.

97. Phillips, *Between Assimilation and Independence*, 66.

98. Peng, *A Taste of Freedom*.

99. Kuo, "The History and Politics of Taiwan's February 28 Incident, 1947–2008," 65–67.

100. Kuo, 74.

101. Harrison, *Legitimacy, Meaning, and Knowledge in the Making of Taiwanese Identity*, 83.

102. Munsterhjelm, *Living Dead in the Pacific*, 22.

103. Kerr, *Formosa Betrayed*, 291.

104. Kuo, "The History and Politics of Taiwan's February 28 Incident," 67.

105. Kuo, 79.

106. Kuo, 77, 89; and Durdin, "Terror in Taiwan," 626–628.

107. Durdin, "Formosa killings are put at 10,000," 6.

108. Durdin, 6.

109. Liao Wen-k`uei (Joshua Liao), *Formosa speaks; the memorandum submitted to the United Nations in September, 1950 in support of the petition for Formosan independence by the Formosan League for Re-emancipation* (Hong Kong: Graphic Press, 1950).

110. National Museum of Taiwan History, Permanent Exhibition placard titled "Striding Towards Democracy."

111. Hutchings, *Time and World Politics*, 64.

112. Beinart, "America needs an entirely new foreign policy for the Trump Age."

113. Zhu, "Why Taiwan is taking a hardline against unification with China – and what that means for the US."

114. For a comparison of Hong Kong's Umbrella Movement with the contemporaneous Sunflower Student Movement in Taiwan, see Ming-sho Ho, *Challenging Beijing's Mandate of Heaven* (Philadelphia: Temple University Press, 2019).

115. For a recent monograph documenting the mass internment of Uyghurs in Xinjiang and the PRC's adoption of the rhetoric and logic of the US-led War on Terror as justification, see Sean R. Roberts, *The War on the Uyghurs: China's Internal Campaign Against a Muslim Minority* (Princeton, NJ: Princeton University Press, 2020).

116. *Hong Kong Free Press* Twitter account, Twitter thread (40 Tweets, 34th Tweet), December 8, 2021, 2:49 a.m.

117. Chou and Tam, "Against One Country, Several Systems."

118. National Museum of Taiwan History, Permanent Exhibition.

Chapter 3

"Chinese Taipei": The Remapping that Explains Taiwan's Geopolitical Predicament

Walking the City

Today, a visitor to Taipei navigates the city, consciously or not, according to a map of China. Upon arriving in Taiwan in 1945, the KMT began a project to rename the Japanese-era streets of Taipei to correspond to toponyms in China and core Confucian and ethnic nationalist ideologies of the ROC. In doing so, the party created a (Republic of) Chinese Taipei, marking their takeover of the city by remaking it in the contours of the metropole.

A tourist wanting a respite from the bustle of the major streets could hardly do better than ducking into the expensively restored Japanese-era wooden houses on the leafy and charming Qingtian Street (Qingtian jie 青田街), in Da'an District (Daan qu 大安區). In recent years, these houses have been converted with the help of government subsidies into trendy art galleries, bookstores, restaurants, and tea shops.[1] Today, these houses are located in the core of Taipei, referred to locally as the "egg yolk district" (*danhuangqu* 蛋黃區), connoting both cartographical centrality and the price and privilege of living there. At mid-century, however, they stood on what was then the eastern, relatively undeveloped edge of the city. The postwar name assigned to this 400-meter-long street corresponds to Qingtian County in Zhejiang Province on the southeastern coast of China. On its northern side, Qingtian Street intersects with Jinhua Street (Jinhua jie 金華街), while four short blocks to its west lies Lishui Street (Lishui jie 麗水街), named for the Zhejiang cities of Jinhua and Lishui.

Just a brisk 45-minute walk west of Qingtian Street brings one to the southwestern borders of China, according to the KMT remapping of the city. The logic of the map breaks down in places. Walking west from Qingtian Street, one continues on to Chaozhou Street (Chaozhou jie 潮州街; named for Chaozhou city in Guangdong Province), which intersects on its western end with Fuzhou Street (Fuzhou jie 福州街; named for Fuzhou city in Fujian Province). In China, however, Chaozhou is to the east of Fuzhou. From Fuzhou Street, one can turn south on Quanzhou Street (Quanzhou jie 泉州街; named for another major coastal port city in Fujian), which faces the Taiwanese city of Taichung across the Strait, and then north onto Zhonghua Road (Zhonghua lu 中華路). *Zhonghua* is often translated into English as "Greater China," a term that defines "China" less according to state borders than ethnicity, culture, and civilization. The concept stretches to potentially include anywhere large populations of Han Chinese and Chinese descendants live, including China proper ("the mainland"), Hong Kong, and Macau, as well as Taiwan and Singapore, and less often, other parts of Southeast Asia. In Bangka District, Taipei's westernmost perimeter, Zhonghua Road takes the visitor north towards Xizang Road (Xizang lu 西藏路), named after the Chinese term for Tibet. As the self-styled successor to the Qing Empire, the ROC claimed the Tibet Area as one of twenty-two provinces in its provisional constitution of 1912, although it only ever managed to exert limited control over the territory, which lay far to the west of the early twentieth-century ROC capitals of Beijing and Nanjing. The east-west route through China is laid out twice on to the topography of Taipei. Walking northward from Xizang Road allows one to mimic an eastward trek through southern China: from Dali Street (Dali jie 大理街; Dali City in Yunnan Province) to Guilin Road (Guilin lu 桂林路; Guilin city in what is now Guangxi Zhuang Autonomous Region), and then to Hengyang Road (Hengyang lu 衡陽路; the city of Hengyangin Hunan Province). To be a flaneur in Taipei is thus to trace, geographically and mnemonically, China in miniature.

Just as New York and New Hampshire in the northeast United States are obvious stand-ins for Yorkshire and Hampshire in Britain, so too are these Taipei streets intended to evoke the originals in China. However, while it is easy to identify European naming practices in the New World as colonial in nature, KMT naming practices in Taiwan have frequently worked towards naturalizing, rather than questioning, the connection between China and Taiwan, promoting a perception of the latter as simply and straightforwardly "Chinese." Using the KMT's makeover of Taipei as a starting point, this chapter shows how the image the ROC created of Taiwan, as both China in microcosm and an essential part of a Chinese nation, is wielded against the Taiwanese today as evidence that they belong to whichever government currently controls "the mainland." It then explores how "Chinese Taipei" became a go-to compromise label in an international system afraid of the ramifications of calling Taiwan "Taiwan." Both as a map that can be traced through the streets of postwar Taipei, and as a name intended to diminish Taiwan, "Chinese Taipei" helps to explain the island's geopolitical predicament and how its people navigate life in what is simultaneously Taiwan, the ROC, and a territory relentlessly coveted by the PRC.

BEFORE "CHINESE TAIPEI"

Before there was a "Chinese Taipei," there were many other versions of Taipei, many other ways of rendering and naming the built environment of the city, as well as the geology and environment that make human life there possible. Taipei is a city built from west to east. The oldest urban neighborhoods (known as Bangka (Mengxia 艋舺) and Tuatiutia (Dadaocheng 大稻埕), in a rough romanization of their names in Taiwanese, are located near the convergence of the Tamsui and Keelung Rivers, before they flow out together in a northwesterly direction towards the Taiwan Strait. Taipei is situated in the flat, bright green lands of the Taipei Basin, which is ringed by densely forested mountains, the volcanic Yangmingshan to the north and Xueshan Range to the south. Nature writer Jessica J. Lee describes the creation of the Taipei Basin as the result of a "slow-motion crumpling of the ground ahead as mountain ranges have advanced. The land dipped, the way a small valley forms at the base of a wave rushing forward."[2]

If the mountains and rivers make one kind of hyper-visible map, encircling and wending their way through the city, geological fault lines carve out a subterranean one, with the Shanchiao Fault forming the southern border and the Taipei Fault the southeastern one. Taipei is a city where nature presses close: during the consecutive weeks of gray rain in the winter (adding up to over two meters of precipitation a year); the muggy, blazing days of summer; the windy, atmospheric disturbance of typhoon season; all punctuated by frequent earthquakes, which with any luck arrive with seconds of warning from a government's early alert system.

The Taipei Basin is the traditional homeland of the Ketagalan plains indigenous people. Han Chinese did not begin settling in the basin until the very late seventeenth century, after the Qing defeat of Koxinga's dynasty and more than half a century after the first significant waves of Chinese settlers arrived in the southwestern coastal plains inhabited by the Siraya. These settlers transformed the Taipei Basin into rice-farming lands. Under Qing rule, the Ketagalan were, like the Siraya, classified as "cooked savages" (*shufan* 熟番), referencing their extensive contact with settlers, in contrast to mountain indigenous tribes labeled as "raw savages" or "uncooked savages" (*shengfan* 生番). Today, efforts to revitalize the Siraya language and gain national recognition have gained much more traction than similar efforts by and for the Ketagalan, whose history, lineage, artifacts, language, and folklore remain notably effaced and understudied.[3]

As anthropologist Tomonori Sugimoto notes, in contrast to "regional" cities, such as Tainan and Taitung, which "often emphasize (if superficially) indigenous heritage in their official discourse" (Siraya and Amis, respectively), Taipei, as the capital and center of development, is instead "almost completely represented as Han space." Since the end of World War II, members of officially recognized indigenous tribes have moved from the central mountains and the east to Taipei and created new communities in the capital. Yet those "who could claim [local] indigeneity, the Ketagalan, are already considered to have been 'assimilated.'" For almost 350 years, settlers and successive governments have "continuously erased" Ketagalan claims and influence in the region.[4]

For three successive governments—Qing, Japanese, and ROC—Taipei served as both a laboratory and a model of modernization, proof of the rightness and legitimacy of their rule. In the nineteenth century, the increase in defense and investment in northern Taiwan was occasioned by challenges confronting Qing rule more broadly. In the wake of the mid-century Opium Wars, China was pressured to establish "treaty ports" for trade with Western merchants on unequal terms. Under the 1858 Treaty of Tientsin, both Tainan in the south and Tamsui in northern Taipei became treaty ports, creating two hubs of international trade and settlement at either end of the island. The Qing also faced territorial encroachment towards the end of the nineteenth century; during the Sino-French War of 1884–1885, French forces unsuccessfully tried to occupy and hold northern Taiwan.

In 1885, Taipei replaced Tainan as the capital city, a status it has retained ever since. Two years later, Taiwan was converted from a prefecture of Fujian into a province in its own right. For six years afterwards, the newly appointed governor of Taiwan Province, Liu Ming-chuan 劉銘傳, undertook a program of defense and infrastructural upgrades, including building an open drainage system in Taipei, the first railway in Taiwan (connecting Keelung, Taipei, and what is now Hsinchu, in the northwest), and the first telegraph line running north to south along the island.[5] With the outbreak of the First Sino-Japanese War in 1894, Taiwan once again became an object of contestation between two regional powers, but this time the Qing was forced by the Treaty of Shimonoseki to cede the island "in perpetuity."

Although the Qing (1683–1895) and Japanese (1895–1945) eras are often treated as separate periods in studies of Taiwan, there are many continuities between the two. Out of the conjuncture of late-Qing crisis and early Japanese colonial rule came modernized systems of state power. For example, the Japanese Government-General inherited the Qing-era community-based system of defense and administration known as the *baojia* 保甲 system, expanding it into the *hoko* system and adding local police stations, with more than a thousand established across the island by 1902. Japanese colonial experimentation was thus melded with Qing-era community-organizing methods into new forms to better understand and exploit Taiwan's population.[6] As the architecture scholar Wu Ping-sheng argues, Liu Ming-chuan's tenure prefigured that of the Japanese chief administrator Goto Shinpei 後藤 新平, who held this role from 1898 to 1905 as a civilian counterpart to the military role of the Japanese Governor-General. Goto described Taiwan as a "colonization university" for Japan, with the intention that it would become the first in a series of colonies in a new, pan-Asian empire.

Much of the layout, construction, and recreational space that was later repurposed to create a "Chinese Taipei" for the Republic of China was conceived of or constructed during the Japanese era. Between

1895 and 1935, the total land included in the Taipei municipality (then called Taihoku) increased nearly fourteen-fold, some three-quarters of it designated as vacant or unsettled land open for development.[7] As described by Joseph Allen in his essayistic examinations of the city, in this period Taipei was transfigured from a traditional Chinese walled city, located in the west of the Basin, to an eastward-looking metropolis with wide, parallel boulevards extending far beyond the original borders of settlement, with the newer neighborhoods intended for Japanese settlers and their families.[8] Along with the West Gate, the city walls—dating from the late Qing era—were dismantled starting in 1904, along with the West Gate. Yet the "displacement" of the previous regime's imprint was only partial. The North, East, South, and Small South Gates were left in place, becoming, in Allen's words, markers of the "absence" of the wall, "fully and blatantly impractical."[9] Today, the East Gate stands awkwardly at the center of a large traffic circle on the main thoroughfare of Zhongshan South Road, facing the Presidential Office and near the Chiang Kai-shek Memorial Hall. The traffic circle was created out of necessity to move cars through the city, with the East Gate no longer marking the end of the city but merely its western third section. Thus are the great ruptures of Taiwan's history turned into everyday features in the lives of Taipei residents.

There was a double logic to these urban redesigns. First, according to architectural scholar Hui-ju Chang, they enabled the Japanese to demonstrate simultaneously their "techno-cultural superiority" over their colonies and their parity with Western Europe and the United States after the shock of Commodore Matthew Perry's forcible opening of Japanese ports in 1853.[10] The new palace (now the Presidential Office of the ROC) overlooking the East Gate built for the Governor-General exemplified these goals. It was the tallest building in Taiwan upon its completion in 1919 and constructed using a blend of European architectural styles, with a central tower and main wings. Second, with the reimagining of the cityscape, Japanese Taihoku became a hub of recreation and aspirational consumption for upwardly mobile segments of the population, both

Taiwanese and Japanese. The 1935 exhibition *Taiwan Exposition: In Commemoration of the First Forty Years of Colonial Rule*—the apex of the city as both a site of display of colonial power and enjoyment for the colonized—was visited by 2.75 million people, many of whom, lured by promotional posters as well as hundreds of thousands of leaflets airdropped from aircraft, arrived in Taihoku by train from central and southern Taiwan,.[11]

The history of one of the main exposition halls—then called the Taihoku Public Auditorium—traces how Japanese Taihoku was remade into "Chinese Taipei" not just as a space where ethnic Chinese settlers lived but a proxy for the idea of a "true China" or else an inalienable and subordinate part of China. During the colonial period, the Taihoku Public Auditorium, clustered with a series of new government buildings and public works projects, was situated close to the Governor General's palace and within the borders of the old Qing-era East Gate. Among the foreign visitors welcomed to the auditorium in 1935 was Chen Yi, then governor of Fujian Province, who had been dispatched by Chiang Kai-shek to represent the ROC at the exposition. In his follow-up reports, Chen spoke approvingly of the high standard of living in Taiwan under Japanese rule and urged that Taiwan be considered as a model for agricultural and industrial development in China.[12] Two years later, Japan would invade China, unleashing a brutal conflict that cost millions of lives.

Upon the end of the war, Chen returned to Taihoku Public Auditorium as the new Governor of Taiwan and head of the new Taiwan Administrative Office to accept the Japanese surrender to the Allied Forces on October 25, 1945, called Retrocession Day, reflecting the official view of the KMT that Taiwan had been "returned" to the ROC. Soon an estimated 384,847 Japanese civilian settlers and their families were relocated to camps in anticipation of repatriation to Japan, while new settlers—bureaucrats, soldiers, businessmen—from China arrived on the island. Concurrently thousands of demobilized Taiwanese who had fought in the Japanese army awaited repatriation from China and Southeast Asia.[13]

The building Chen Yi visited for the Taiwan Exposition and where he accepted Japan's surrender a decade later was renamed Taipei Zhongshan Hall (Taibei zhongshan tang 台北中山堂), after the honorific title given to the revolutionary leader Sun Yat-sen.[14]

One can still visit Zhongshan Hall today. In the crescent-shaped plaza facing the hall stands a monument to the Victory in the War Against Japan and the Retrocession of Taiwan, dedicated in 2011 to the 100th anniversary of the establishment of the ROC. Running along the bottom of a large stone wall is a timeline with just three years—1895, 1937, and 1945—carved in, referring to the Treaty of Shimonoseki, the start of the Second Sino-Japanese War, and the end of World War II, respectively. The timeline limits the visitor's understanding of Taiwanese history to just fifty years. A dedicatory plaque in front of the wall asserts that Japan's invasion of Chinese territory began not in 1937 but 1895 and pays tribute to the small minority of Taiwanese who volunteered to fight against Imperial Japan on the side of the ROC, to "protect the motherland and recover Taiwan" (*baowei zuguo, shoufu Taiwan* 保衛祖國，收復台灣). In addition to drawing a connection between anti-Japanese activists and fighters from Taiwan and people living in China in the 1930s, the text emphasizes the world historical role of the ROC in co-founding the League of Nations in 1919 and partnering with English, American, and Soviet Allies in World War II.[15] Together, the renaming of the building and the monument timeline treat Japanese Taihoku as an aberration, a theft from the ROC—not just the Qing—that was finally righted on Retrocession Day.

Cutting the timeline at 1945 diverts the viewer's attention away not only from Japanese Taihoku but also from a Taiwanese Taipei, born in the self-rule movements of the 1920s, briefly resurgent following the war, and then suppressed by the new ROC government. Chen Yi was not only the admiring ROC delegate to the 1935 Taiwan Exposition and the triumphant new governor taking command of Taiwan on behalf of the Allies in 1945. He was also the official who wired to Nanjing for soldiers to put down the uprising that began on February 28, 1947. Taiwanese community leaders had quickly formed February 28 Settlement Committees across the island to restore order and address grievances over economic mismanagement, corruption, and the monopolization of state positions by the "mainlander" newcomers. Joined by student representatives from area universities, the Taipei Settlement Committee met on March 2, 1947, at Zhongshan Hall to discuss their demands of Chen's administration, a meeting whose occurrence and aftermath belie the narrative that retrocession constituted a harmonious closure of a historical wound.[16] On March 8, less than a week after Chen gave the settlement committee his word that he would not take military action against the Taiwanese, additional ROC troops landed at the northern port city of Keelung and the southern city of Kaohsiung and began killing thousands of civilians.

The actions of the 228 Settlement Committee go unmentioned in the plaques that now sit outside Zhongshan Hall. However, one can walk a mere three minutes east of the hall down Hengyang Road to the 228 Peace Memorial Park. The park was opened in 1900 as Taihoku New Park, the first urban recreational park planned by the Japanese. Within the grounds is a museum building that once housed the state-run radio broadcast station. On February 28, 1947, protestors stormed the station to broadcast reports of the widow's beating in Tuatutia and rally sympathizers in and outside of Taipei. At the heart of the park, next to the museum, stands a memorial to the victims of 228 that was consecrated in 1997. The memorial was designed by architect Cheng Tzu-tsai 鄭自才, who as a young man in his thirties on a visit to New York City in April 1970, staged an unsuccessful assassination attempt of Chiang Ching-kuo, at the time Vice Premier of the ROC. Cheng was arrested by New York police and bailed out for $95,000, raised by the diasporic Taiwanese community, before fleeing to Sweden and ultimately being extradited back to the US to spend five years in prison. In 1991, Cheng returned to Taiwan from the US for his father's funeral and was arrested for illegal entry as a blacklisted dissident, becoming one of the last political prisoners of the martial law and pre-democratic era in Taiwan. He submitted his winning design for the 228 Peace Memorial from jail in Kaohsiung.[17]

Zhongshan Hall and 228 Peace Memorial Park are historical sites that express the overlapping realities that Taiwanese people inhabit as a (post)colonial society, as both the Republic of China and Taiwan. Both the hall and the park were built as part of Japanese modernization projects, and both served as major exhibition sites for the 1935 Taiwan Exposition. Both saw their roles as sites of assembly and communication quickly appropriated by the incoming ROC, and both became important landmarks of negotiation and resistance by Taipei residents responding to the crisis of KMT governance of Taiwan after 1945.

Yet the stories told by the memorials erected on their respective grounds are exclusive of one another, one celebrating the "return" of Taiwan to the ROC, the other in remembrance of the violence that the ROC military enacted on its Taiwanese citizens soon afterwards. One naturalizes a "Chinese Taipei" that is part of a greater Chinese nation known as the Republic of China, while the other challenges it, calling attention to the killings ordered by the KMT regime to maintain control of Taiwan. One site glorifies the epoch-defining role of the ROC, modern republican successor to the Qing empire that briefly united the two sides of the Strait under a single government. The other site offers a history of events silenced for forty years until their acknowledgement in the late 1980s helped spur the island's transformation into a modern democracy.

Today, it is the 228 Peace Park, rather than Zhongshan Hall, that occupies a greater role in Taipei's public and political life. The plausibility of the KMT's claim to be the legitimate governor of a cross-Strait "one China" continued to diminish, as its exile to Taiwan stretched into its fifth decade and the upper ranks of the party were opened to people born in Taiwan. The end of martial law in 1987, the revision of anti-sedition laws in 1991, and the subsequent democratization of the political system made room for, and were propelled by, the expression of a distinctively Taiwanese identity. This identity has been expressed, among many other ways, in the repurposing and renaming of this park. In part by memorializing the terrible events of 1947, the people of Taiwan have come to know themselves as a modern democratic society, rendering the vision of a "reunification" with another authoritarian Chinese government untenable.[18]

MAKING 'CHINESE TAIPEI'

The KMT built "Chinese Taipei" both by repurposing the architecture of Japanese Taihoku and by undertaking new construction projects to bolster the party's standing as the rightful ruler of China. Shortly after Retrocession Day in 1945, the Taiwan Provincial Administrative Office instructed local governments to develop proposals for renaming the streets in their jurisdictions. Japanese names were to be replaced with Chinese ones that promoted the "ethnic Chinese spirit," Confucian ideals, and the Three Principles of the People. Then in January 1947, the Provincial Administrative Office unveiled an additional blueprint for the city of Taipei, designed by Shanghai-born architect Cheng Ting-pang 鄭定邦, that would superimpose a rough map of China onto the city's existing neighborhoods, drawing on a similar mid-nineteenth century redesign of Shanghai. Taiwan studies scholar Peter Kang calculates that

> About 70% of [Taipei] streets [now] bore place names from China... This came at the expense of local geographies or habits, the use of which dropped considerably, from 83% of all street names in 1946 to less than 7% in 1947...the symbolic landscape of postwar Taipei turned out to be a terrain which manifested the nationalistic geography of China.[19]

The lived experience of Taiwanese was thus overlaid by a map of Republican China that carried contested historical, geographical, and emotional reference points. With its defeat in the Chinese Civil War in 1949, the KMT proclaimed that it would transform Taiwan into an exemplar for all of China. The policy created two realities. Under the ROC state, Taiwan was supposed to be a model of KMT economic development, demonstrating the party's ideological and instrumental superiority over the rival CCP but also, in a literal sense, it was meant to mimic the map of China in its urban streetscapes, so that the people of Taiwan could be said to be living in China, and thus to belong to it. The Great Exodus of 1949 also made Taipei demographically more Chinese than the rest of the island. Approximately 1.2 million people, about half of them military men, fled from China to Taiwan in the five-year period just before and after the end of the Chinese Civil War, ultimately comprising 14% of Taiwan's population by mid-century. In 1965, of the twenty-two townships, villages, and districts where the proportion of "mainlanders" (*waishengren*) surpassed 30% of the local population, eleven were within Taipei city or county.[20] Today, to use Taiwan's color-coded political parlance, the capital still tends to vote "blue" in favor of the KMT whereas the south typically votes "green" in favor of the DPP.[21]

After moving to Taiwan, the KMT allocated resources in the form of jobs, pensions, and housing by provincial origin in ways that strongly favored *waishengren* over *benshengren* (pre-1945 settlers) and indigenous Taiwanese. As political scientist Pei-te Lien notes, the highest offices in both the government and military held almost exclusively by *waishengren*. "A de facto racist quota was in place [until 1990] when only 5 percent of civil service slots," which came with generous retirement pensions, "were allocated for Taiwanese, who constituted at least 85 percent of the population of the island. The rationale was that the population of Taiwan was only 5 percent of the Chinese population and Taiwan was [only] one of the Chinese provinces."[22]

Still, there was great variation in the living conditions assigned to or reserved for *waishengren*. Da'an District, where Qingtian Street is located, was recorded as being 66.1% *waishengren* in that same 1965 survey.[23] Its postwar history exemplifies the socioeconomic diversity that existed within what was, for political and practical reasons, treated as a single ethnic group by a party-state that relied on their support. Some of the

elegant colonial-era homes on Qingtian Street that had once housed
Japanese civil servants or professors at the nearby Taihoku University
were now taken over by their *waishengren* counterparts and the school
itself renamed National Taiwan University.[24]

Barely half a kilometer to the east, however, thousands of poor *waishengren* and their families lived in two *juancun* built on land originally
set aside by Japanese authorities in 1932 for a new municipal park. In
1994, a park was finally inaugurated on the site after the demolition of
the *juancun* and the removal of the remaining residents. Today, Da'an
Forest Park (Daan senlin gongyuan 大安森林公園) sits at the center of
some of the most expensive real estate in Taipei. The redevelopment
of the area has also erased local memory, as the most visible reminders
of the (self-)segregation and separate status of *waishengren* give way to
the more prosaic profit motives of property developers. In December
2019, the *United Daily News* (Lianhe bao聯合報), a newspaper that often
supports the KMT, posted on their Facebook page a photo of the cramped
juancun that once stood on the park land, eliciting astonishment from
readers. One netizen responded, "I've lived in Taipei thirty years and
only now am I learning about this!"[25] In October 2020, part of this history
was reconstructed when an architectural firm, archicake design, built
a small iron-framed house in the park, a replica in size and shape of a
typical *juancun* dwelling (six *ping* 坪, or barely 20 square meters) as an
art installation that doubled up as a memorial. Inside the structure sat a
single, flimsy chair and built into the opposite wall was the outline of the
ROC flag, testifying to both the poverty of the former residents and the
loyalty they showed towards the party that had placed them on this plot
of land and would eventually help evict them from it. An accompanying
plaque relayed the memories of second generation *waishengren* who
had grown up in the *juancun*: " ...every night at dusk, there were shouts
in various provincial languages calling children to come home..."[26] On
occasion, local movements have sprung up to preserve *juancun* from
being demolished in what are now high-cost, high-demand areas, such as
44 South Village (Si si nan cun 四四南村) near the Taipei 101 skyscraper,

which has been repurposed as a museum and art exhibition space and is popular with wedding photographers looking for what is now considered nostalgic charm.

CREATING A TAIWANESE TAIPEI

If the postwar city had to be Sinicized in the specific image of the Republic of China, stripped of its reminders of Japanese cultural and linguistic influence, so too did its residents. The 1946–1947 remapping of Taipei had the effect of distancing city residents from their immediate surroundings and from the ways of knowing, naming, and speaking that had existed before KMT occupation. The new compulsory school curriculum did the same, teaching the history and geography of China to students while treating Taiwan as a temporary inferior substitute for the real China and yet paradoxically important as a model "province" to signal to the PRC the success of KMT rule.

For two generations from 1945 to 1997, attending school in Taiwan meant learning very little about Taiwan itself. As cultural studies scholar Bi-yu Chang observes, "the concept of 'Taiwan' in geography text-books was constructed from the perspective of 'outsiders', i.e., main-landers...Taiwanese students were treated as 'Chinese diaspora' and promised a Chinese motherland one day."[27] The schooling the Taiwanese students received was thus supposed to create an artificial sense of "indignation...about being a shamed and exiled people" and to reconcile them to the military service that awaited them when they became young adults.[28] During this period, the KMT leadership constantly proclaimed its goal to "reconquer the mainland," but the only new supply of military recruits available were young men born and raised in Taiwan, over-whelmingly from families that had not participated in the Chinese Civil War.[29] Education and military service were directed at the ideological goal of representing and controlling all of China, but in the face of geopolitical reality, these goals reduced ultimately to a logic of state power over Taiwan only, for which control itself was the purpose.

Having grown up in this total system, Taiwanese from their late thirties to mid seventies of all ethnic and linguistic backgrounds know by heart the dynasties of China and can recite some Tang-era poetry from memory. They were taught that the true capital of "their country" was Nanjing, the capital of China under ROC control. They learned that "their country's" highest peak was Mount Everest, bordered by Tibet and Nepal, not the central Taiwanese peak called Jade Mountain (Yushan 玉山) and known as Batongguan 八通關 or Patungkuanu in the Tsou indigenous language. They learned that the longest river in their "home" was the Yangtze River in China, not the Zhoushui River (Zhoushui xi 濁水溪), called "Lô-chúi-khoe" in Taiwanese, which flowed from the heart of the island westward out to the Taiwan Strait. These students had to pay fines and wear dunce caps and shame boards for speaking Taiwanese, Hakka, or indigenous languages in school. The Taiwanese, as sociologist Chin-ju Mao notes, "resented being caught between an abstract notion of a remote China, about which they learned much, and a concrete reality in Taiwan, about which they learned too little, or were not allowed to learn."[30] These everyday instances of punitive, bullying state power became indelibly marked on generations of Taiwanese. Part of the impetus for the social movements of the 1970s and 1980s that drove democratization was a curiosity about what was "local" (*bentu* 本土) and authentically Taiwanese, and hence stigmatized or forbidden.

The map of Taipei as map of China helps to explain the tragedies of Taiwan's modern history and the overlapping geopolitical realities Taiwanese people inhabit as both Taiwan and the Republic of China. But the changes and additions to the city map in the last three decades show Taiwanese society's fitful, contested, and creative efforts at decolonization and national self-determination in a wide range of areas, such as law, policy, urban development, and public life. These continue as the party responsible for the authoritarian era still plays a prominent role in politics and another Chinese party-state remains fixated on annexing Taiwan, likely reimplementing the same kind of abuses. Democratization and the reclaiming of Taipei are conjoined processes. The first formal efforts to dismantle the personality cult of Chiang Kai-shek and rename major sites of the KMT cityscape was the work of a key figure in Taiwan's democratic politics, Chen Shui-bian of the DPP. In 1994, Chen, the son of Taiwanese-speaking tenant farmers from Tainan County, became both the first popularly elected mayor of Taipei since 1967 and the first from a party other than the KMT. The city had been designated a special administrative region by Chiang Kai-shek in 1967 to allow the ROC government to appoint its mayors. Chen took office in the new city hall built in Xinyi District as part of the protracted development of eastern Taipei. The development signaled the redistribution of political power away from the national-level institutions in the center of the city, a process that began under Chen's predecessor, Lee Teng-hui.

Trained as a lawyer, Chen Shui-bian was part of a cohort of high-profile dissidents under Chiang Ching-kuo, in the latter days of the White Terror. He entered politics by agreeing to serve as a defense attorney for the publisher Huang Hsin-chieh 黃信介, one of the organizers of a pro-democracy demonstration in the southern port city of Kaohsiung on December 10, 1979. Huang and his fellow defendants, including Chen's future vice president Annette Lu 呂秀蓮, were held at the Jingmei Military Detention Center (Jingmei junshi kanshousuo景美軍事看守所), located near the confluence of the Xindian and Jingmei Rivers in southwest Taipei. The torture the defendants endured in custody, the lengthy sentences handed down (Huang received fourteen years), the brilliant courtroom performances by the defense lawyers like Chen, and the opening of the trials to international news coverage all contributed to the making of the so-called Kaohsiung Incident a tipping point in the end of the White Terror and the start of the transition to democracy.[31] Hsiau A-chin argues that this generation of *dangwai* activists began renarrating its understanding of Taiwanese history in the crucible of the 1980s, coming to see their work as part of a long struggle for Taiwanese self-determination stretching back to the middle of the Japanese colonial period.[32]

Six years after he was elected mayor, in 2000, Chen Shui-bian would become the first non-KMT president of the ROC, winning 39 percent of the vote in a three-way race. As an open advocate of Taiwanese identity and sovereignty, he served as the executive of a state long hostile to both. His two terms necessarily became a critical test of Taiwan's developing democratic institutions. During his eight years as president, the KMT held onto a majority in the legislature and KMT party chair Lien Chan 連戰 opened party-to-party talks with CCP chair Hu Jintao 胡錦濤, united in their shared antipathy to actions perceived as "separating" Taiwan from their respective versions of China.

Chen pressed on with a parallel policy of "Taiwanization" in state institutions. These included printing the name "Taiwan" in English on ROC passports starting in 2003, changing the names of state-owned publications and corporations from "China" to "Taiwan" where he was able to, and forcing the National Unification Council (Guojia tongyi weiyuanhui 國家統一委員會), whose remit was promoting the smooth reintegration of "the mainland" with the ROC, into abeyance in 2006.[33] After two more peaceful transfers of the executive position later—from Chen to his KMT successor Ma Ying-jeou 馬英九 in 2008, and then from Ma back to the DPP's Tsai Ing-wen in 2016—it can be difficult to convey just how divisive Chen's terms were, and how much pushback using "Taiwan" in place of "the ROC" as a state identity generated.

Written into the urban life of Taipei, the legacy of the authoritarian period is visible in democratic Taiwan in how much of the conventional tourist information is still oriented around sites built by the KMT in the 1960s and 1970s to glorify the ROC and its early leaders. These include the National Palace Museum, which houses priceless artifacts from the Forbidden City that the party took when they fled from China, and the Chiang Kai-shek Memorial Hall (Guoli zhongzheng jinian tang 國立中正紀念堂), the imposing blue-and-white octagonal monument housing a 6.3-meter bronze statue of a benevolently smiling Chiang. As literary scholar Kirk Denton notes, "Most of [the] museums [built before the end of martial law] were clustered in and around the Taipei area, the capital of the 'province' and the center of KMT power, leaving the rest of Taiwan a relative museum vacuum."[34]

A tourist itinerary based instead on alterations to the urban landscape that began in the 1990s under Chen as mayor and later as president gives a vivid sense of Taipei not as "Chinese Taipei" but as a city of protest and democratic reform, with a history that remains contested. Those changes in the urban landscape direct attention to generational changes in Taiwanese identity amidst what historian Albert Wu describes as the "inversion of China and Taiwan's economic and geopolitical position."[35] In this way, the political events through which democratic Taiwan was fought for have been made visible in Taiwan's everyday urban life, and whose normalization and institutionalization continues.

In 2007, during Chen's second term as president, the former Jingmei Military Detention Center was dedicated as a human rights museum, in honor of Huang, Lu, and the thousands of other lesser-known dissidents held there. Years later, in August 2022, US Speaker of the House Nancy Pelosi would spend an afternoon at the Jingmei White Terror Memorial Park (Baise kongbu jingmei jinian yuanqu 白色恐怖景美紀念園區) in the company of human rights activists from China and Taiwan during her visit to Taiwan.

In 2007, too, Chen renamed the expansive plaza surrounding the Chiang Kai-shek Memorial Hall in Taipei as Liberty Square (Ziyou guangchang 自由廣場), commemorating its role as a site of mass protest and activism during Taiwan's democratic transition in the late 1980s. After Chiang Ching-kuo's death on January 13, 1988, a faction of elite waishengren tried to block the succession of his handpicked vice president Lee Teng-hui, fearing that Lee would undermine the cause of KMT conservatives.[36] In the leadup to Lee's inauguration in 1990, after he had been formally appointed as president of the ROC by the 712 members of National Assembly, 632 of whom "represented" the provinces of China, the Chiang Kai-shek Memorial was taken over by a six-day sit-in in

March by students that became known as the Wild Lily Movement. At its height, more than 20,000 students camped out in the plaza and occupied the steps of the memorial, chanting, "Why do you keep lying to the people? Why must democracy always remain in the future?"[37] At the entrance to the protest, they constructed a towering replica of a Formosan Wild Lily, an indigenous flower that symbolized their demands for political localization: the abolition of the legal machinery of martial law, the dissolution of the National Assembly, and direct elections for the legislature, presidency, and vice presidency.

Like the leaders of China who had met with student protesters in Tiananmen Square in 1989, Lee met with the leaders of the Wild Lily Movement. Unlike the Chinese leaders, who initiated a military crackdown of the Beijing protesters, Lee responded peacefully to the demands of the White Lilies. The provisions that formed the legal basis of martial law were rescinded in 1991, the first direct elections for the Legislative Yuan held in 1992, and the National Assembly was stripped of its role in choosing the president and vice president in 1994 before being abolished altogether in 2005.[38] In the first free elections for the executive held in 1996, Lee won against the DPP candidate, Peng Ming-min, who had spent the1960s and 1970s in exile for his advocacy against the dictatorship. Scholars of democratization regard this halting process—which transformed civic and social life in Taiwan and led to substantial reform of the Republic of China government, rather than its overthrow—as a "political miracle" and a rare success story of peaceful democratic transition.

In the decades after the Wild Lily Movement, Taipei has become a site onto which the KMT (pan-blue) and DPP (pan-green) project their competing political visions, using the urban fabric available to them. The cityscape, like a dense text, is now crowded with contradictory statements about Taiwan's relationship to China and its future with or apart from "the mainland." Under Chen's administration, the Chiang Kai-shek Memorial Hall itself was also renamed to the National Taiwan Democracy Memorial Hall (Guoli Taiwan minzhu jinian guan 國立臺灣民主紀念

館). In 2008, during the last weeks of Chen's second presidential term, the memorial hall space itself was turned into a democracy exhibition, featuring displays of images of protest actions and manifestos against Chiang's rule. The military honor guard for the statue was suspended. After the DPP's defeat and election of the KMT's Ma Ying-jeou that year, the name of the hall was returned to the original Chiang Kai-shek Memorial Hall, the exhibition removed, and the honor guard restored. Thus, just as Taipei Zhongshan Hall and the 228 Peace Memorial Park lie adjacent in the cityscape, Chiang Kai-shek Memorial Hall was left sitting within Liberty Square, signaling towards the continuing fight over how the city is named and framed.

The long debate about the Chiang Kai-shek Memorial Hall has also obscured the costs of a "political miracle" that emphasized gradualism and harmony over accountability for perpetrators. The Transitional Justice Committee, established by Tsai Ing-wen and active from May 2018 to May 2022, recommended that the bronze statue of Chiang—the "axis of worship"—be removed and that the memorial be completely redesigned to make more inviting and accessible the "unfriendly and closed-off atmosphere, which preserves and even commemorates autocratic ruler-ship."[39] When the committee issued its report, columnist Michael Turton remarked, "It is 2021. Not a single person has been punished for the thousands of dead, for those tortured and imprisoned and exiled, for five decades of authoritarian control…Our democratic transition remains, as Naiteh Wu wrote in 2005, a transition without justice."[40]

The *dangwai* activists of the 1980s and the Wild Lilies of the 1990s lived to see the ROC evolve from a one-party dictatorship into a multiparty democracy, but they have yet to see Taiwan welcomed into the international system. Some continued to advocate for the complete abolition of the ROC. Others adjusted to the reality of increasing PRC threat by arguing that the ROC had become a kind of hybrid nation, one they referred to as "ROC-Taiwan" or "ROC (Taiwan)". They set aside the question of declaring a *de jure* Republic of Taiwan, focusing instead on expanding Taiwanese people's international space under any name.

In today's Taipei, the *benshengren*, Taiwanese-language consciousness that fueled a considerable part of the democracy movement has come to be regarded by some as exclusionary and ethnocentric. Taiwanese identity is now claimed by a people with a diversity of family backgrounds and political views and tested by newly visible communities, such as new immigrants (*xinzhumin*新住民) and LGBTQI+ Taiwanese. Furthermore, the success of the KMT's linguicidal policies means that young people today, who overwhelmingly identify as Taiwanese, often cannot express that identity in Taiwanese Hokkien or any language except Mandarin. Then, too, Taiwan's experience of rapid postwar economic development and its critical role in contemporary supply chains, became raw material for identities that could not easily be reduced to pan-blue or pan-green. The iconic Taipei 101 skyscraper, for example (another legacy of the Lee Teng-hui and Chen Shui-bian eras), serves as the centerpiece of countless promotional activities for Taiwan. It dominates the eastern skyline of the city, developed in the last decades of the twentieth century, representing a city shaped by urban modernization in the recognizable forms of global capital and consumer culture.

Millennial Taiwanese identity is largely articulated in Mandarin and more indifferent to the ethnic designations of mid-century, thus differing in key ways from previous iterations of "Taiwaneseness". It has nonetheless generated its own landmark protests, most notably the Sunflower Student Movement of 2014, which opposed the seeming rapprochement of the KMT and CCP, against the backdrop of anxieties generated by the PRC's economic and military rise. In the local parlance, this is a generation "born independent," with no memory of a time before the end of martial law. They passed through a revised social studies curriculum, anchored by the textbook series *Knowing Taiwan* (*Renshi Taiwan* 認識台灣), introduced in September 1997, that centered their education on Taiwan and not an imagined Republic of China.[41] "Even more significantly," writer Nicholas Haggerty argues, "they came of age while Chen [Shui-bian] was politicizing public life with campaigns for Taiwan's nationhood and international status."[42]

The future Sunflowers cut their teeth on activism in the late 2000s and early 2010s. At the start of Ma Ying-jeou's first presidential term in 2008, the Wild Strawberries Movement (Ye caomei yundong 野草莓運動) sprang up to protest a visit to Taiwan by Chen Yunlin 陳雲林, then-chairman of China's pro-unification Association for Relations Across the Taiwan Strait (ARATS) . The name of the movement was a challenge to the pejorative label "strawberries" that was sometimes applied to young Taiwanese to mean sweet but easily bruised. Later, in 2012, another key campaign known as the Anti-Media Monopoly Movement (Fan Meiti Longduan Yundong 反媒體壟斷運動) challenged the buy-out of the China Times Media Group by Want Want Holdings, a snack food producer with deep commercial interests in China.

On March 14, 2014, a group of students, drawn from participants in these earlier movements, broke into the legislature and staged an occupation to block the KMT majority from passing a Cross-Strait Services Trade Agreement (CSSTA), a free trade agreement which would have allowed Chinese companies greater market access to commercial services in Taiwan like banking, construction, tourism, publishing, and communications.[43] This developing Sunflower Movement (Taiyanghua xueyun 太陽花學運) highlighted that for the generation aged twenty to thirty-five, the authoritarian specter was no longer the single-party ROC but the economically and geopolitically dominant PRC, which had to be repeatedly outmaneuvered to preserve the status quo of a democratic Taiwan.

A core group of students held the legislative building for twenty-three days until April 10. In a fateful decision, the Legislative Speaker, Wang Jin-pyng 王金平 of the KMT, declined to order the police into the chambers. The protestors toyed with the ROC emblems of the legislature through their Taiwan-focused messaging. Around the large portrait of

Sun Yat-sen and the ROC flag that hang at the front of the chambers, they placed posters and banners reading "Free Taiwan," "God Bless Taiwan," and "Taiwan is not for sale." Below Sun's portrait they placed a drawing of Nylon Deng (Cheng Nan-jung 鄭南榕), the martyr for free speech who self-immolated in his office in Taipei on April 7, 1989, instead of allowing himself to be arrested on charges of insurrection for printing a constitution for a prospective "Republic of Taiwan." As the hours ticked away, counted on a makeshift timer appended to the bottom of Sun's portrait, the students held their own policy discussion sessions and created their own makeshift government, carnivalesque and utopian in nature.[44] Nonetheless, among their formal demands, they did not call for the abolition of the ROC or the declaration of a *de jure* Republic of Taiwan, instead keeping their attention focused more narrowly on the CSSTA. But the end of the protest, they had secured a promise from Speaker Wang to postpone the trade agreement indefinitely.

The legislative occupation was supported by an encampment outside, creating a spontaneous political infrastructure parallel to the formal systems of the ROC. Supporters gathered day and night to hold teach-ins and broadcast events through social media. Protesters included a florist whose spontaneous donation of sunflower blooms lent the nascent movement its name. The flower was said to represent the sunlight of democracy shining into the "black box" of the secret negotiations between Taipei and Beijing for the CSSTA. But whether the Sunflowers had prevented democratic corrosion by thwarting a bill giving state-backed Chinese corporations outsized influence in the Taiwanese market, or flouted bedrock democratic norms by blocking the majority KMT legislature from advancing its agenda, was the subject of vigorous debate in Taiwan and among the Taiwanese diaspora.

During the occupation, on March 30, student leader Lin Fei-fan 林飛帆 led supporters on a solidarity march on Ketagalan Boulevard, an eight-lane road facing the grand Japanese-colonial-era Presidential Office. Barricaded at the center of state power, he pointed towards a site that subverted the party's postwar mapping of the city. Ketagalan Boulevard, like Liberty Square, was renamed on Chen Shui-bian's initiative in 1996 when he was mayor of Taipei. The KMT had called it Chieh-shou Road (Jie shou lu 介壽路), which translates into "Long live Chiang Kai-shek." Chen's rededication honored the Ketagalan plains indigenous people, instrumentalizing their history to discredit the idea that Taiwan was the property of the ROC. When Lin made his rallying call eighteen years later, an estimated half a million people turned out on Ketagalan Boulevard and the surrounding streets in response. As geographer Ian Rowen points out, it was the largest student uprising in Asia at the time (occurring six months before the Umbrella Movement broke out in Hong Kong) and, according to sociologist Ming-sho Ho, the "largest protest-based mobilization in Taiwan's history."[45]

In the years since, the Sunflower Movement has had a significant impact on Taiwanese and regional politics. Although the Sunflowers had deliberately rejected any association with the DPP during their occupation, in its wake in 2016 the KMT lost both the presidency and, for the first time, the legislature, a scenario which was repeated in 2020. With Tsai Ing-wen's election in 2016, Beijing cut off official contact with Taipei and restarted its campaign to pressure the few states that still recognized the ROC to switch ties, successfully reducing the number from nineteen to fifteen between 2017 and 2019. The Sunflower activists also entered politics themselves, with some founding "third force" leftist and center-left parties like the New Power Party (NPP) and Social Democratic Party (SDP, Shehui minzhu dang 社會民主黨) that aimed to transcend the blue-green binary, while Lin Fei-fan joined the DPP and became a deputy secretary-general of the party.[46]

For a brief period, the Sunflowers, like the Wild Lilies before them, transformed the center of Taipei into a mass, free-ranging, and accessible discussion on Taiwanese democracy. Unlike the Wild Lilies, the Sunflowers have not had a public gathering space in Taipei officially renamed after them. Their legacy is both more recent and ambiguous than that of the Wild Lilies. They were not protesting for baseline democratic rights like universal suffrage or the legalization of opposition parties but against policies advocated by duly elected legislators that would have increased the economic integration of the Chinese and Taiwanese markets. Democracy is widely celebrated today in Taiwan as a public good and a cornerstone of Taiwanese identity. Democracy alone, however, can provide no simple path out of the existential dilemma posed by the PRC. Today, further undoing "Chinese Taipei" in favor of a Taiwanese Taipei and Taiwanese Taiwan comes with a greater geopolitical risk. It would not only unsettle the ever-more spectral presence of the ROC but also upset a powerful PRC with its eyes fixated on Taiwan. Thus, "Chinese Taipei" remains in place in the infrastructure and design of Taipei City, a projection of an imagined motherland that is simultaneously lost and immanently threatening to the full realization of a Taiwanese Taipei.

"Chinese Taipei" at the Olympics and beyond

"Chinese Taipei" is in some ways a real place: a city whose planning, construction, and partial deconstruction traces the fate of the KMT and modern Chinese republican nationalism itself. More often, it is heard in the context of (mis)naming Taiwan in the international sphere. As such, it is disliked by many Taiwanese who regard it as a belittling label, a reminder of Taiwan's historic and continuing marginalization.

On July 23, 2021, during the opening ceremony for the delayed Tokyo Olympics, Taiwanese social media lit up at the phrase "It's Taiwan!" (*Taiwan desu* 「台湾です」), which the Japanese broadcaster NHK announced as the team from Taiwan entered the stadium, bearing a flag with the emblem of a white sun on a circular blue background, sitting atop the interlocking Olympic rings.[47] This was the flag of the "Chinese Taipei Olympic Team," the name that athletes from Taiwan have had to compete under since 1981.

This statement "It's Taiwan!" functioned in two ways in the opening ceremony: first, it informed audiences watching in the stadium and at home where the athletes holding this flag hailed from, and second, it acknowledged the absurdity of referring to the Taiwanese team by the name "Chinese Taipei." In another, subtler gesture, the Japanese Olympic Committee assigned the team to enter the stadium just ahead of Tajikistan, according to the spelling of "Taiwan" in the katakana alphabet.

Like so many other aspects of the global discourse about Taiwan, the label "Chinese Taipei" - intended to placate Beijing instead stirs up questions and answers that end up pointing back to Taiwan's de facto sovereignty. While NHK made a simple, declarative statement, broadcasters from other countries provided more historical context. Seven Network from Australia, for instance, noted that the team was participating as "Chinese Taipei *here*" and proceeded to offer a quick history lesson: "It's competed under all sorts of various names: the Republic of China in '56; Taiwan Formosa in '60; Taiwan from '64 to '72; and Chinese Taipei from 1984 onwards."[48]

Contained within this timeline were hints at alternative histories, ones that might have led Taiwan not to its present diplomatic isolation but its international recognition as a Taiwanese, not Chinese, nation. The 1956 Melbourne Summer Olympics were the first year that the Republic of China (ROC) government fielded a team in the games since its self-exile to Taiwan in 1949. The International Olympic Committee (IOC) also recognized a committee from the PRC, but the ROC decided to boycott the event over this "two Chinas" policy. In 1960, the IOC decided that the ROC team could only participate in the Rome Summer Olympics as "Formosa" (the name that sixteenth-century Portuguese sailors gave to Taiwan), thus reflecting the territory that its government actually administered. The team marched in the opening ceremony carrying a large banner that read "Under Protest," insisting that "Formosa" was not a country in itself but merely a part of the true China, the ROC.[49] At the time, this was the only permissible opinion on Taiwan's status that could be expressed publicly within the island itself. "Formosa" was the commonly-used name for the island in English before World War II. In the 1960s and 1970s, it became the preferred nomenclature of dissidents, democracy activists, and Taiwanese nationalists, and as such it was anathema to the KMT regime.

Thus, like the United Nations, the World Trade Organization, and even the Miss World Organization, the IOC initially tried to work out agreements that would allow representatives from both the PRC and ROC to take part in international forums.[50] Prior to the 1976 Montreal Summer Olympics, Canadian prime minister Pierre Trudeau tried to pressure the ROC Olympic Committee to compete as "Taiwan" but was rebuffed by Chiang Ching-kuo.[51] Then in 1979, the IOC passed the Nagoya Resolution, which invented a new team name—Chinese Taipei—for athletes holding ROC citizenship.[52] It used the city name "Taipei" as a synecdoche for the whole of Taiwan and its outlying islands, attempting to find a compromise between the ideological demands of both Beijing and the authoritarian KMT government based in Taipei.

The white sun on a blue background featured on the Chinese Taipei Olympic Flag is the party emblem of the KMT. Its inclusion points to the fact that when decisions were being made in the UN and IOC to switch recognition of "China" from the ROC to the PRC, Taiwan was still under unelected single-party rule. Shortly after Chiang Ching-kuo's death, leading up to Taiwan's transition to multiparty democracy, the KMT abandoned its outlandish goal of "retaking the mainland" at its 1988 party congress. Still, the decisions of both Chiang dictators and the CCP had already shut the people of Taiwan out from representation in major international organizations, in addition to normalizing language that marginalized Taiwan.

The Olympics highlights how Taiwan's existence destabilizes the very language used to describe it. It also exposes the limitations, hypocrisies, and absurdities of an international system that professes liberal ideas of inclusion but bows to the preferences of a few powerful and wealthy nation-states. The reality of a democratic Taiwanese state today, with its own geopolitical and civic identity, challenges the narratives about an indivisible China put forth by the CCP. Simultaneously, terms like "Chinese Taipei" reveal how the global community has accommodated these same narratives as a concession to Chinese state power.

Today, a decision by the IOC to allow athletes to compete as "Taiwan" or even "Formosa" would likely be met with widespread pride and excitement at home, reflecting a tidal shift in self-identification post-democratization. In 2018, activists gathered enough signatures to add a referendum to the ballots that November, which asked voters to agree or disagree on "the use of [the name] 'Taiwan' when participating in all international sport competitions, including the 2020 Tokyo Olympics." The measure was ultimately rejected by 54.8% of voters, the defeat hinging in part on public fear that its passage would lead to Taiwanese athletes being banned from the Olympics by the IOC, in deference to the PRC.[53]

Still, the unexpectedly strong showing of the Chinese Taipei team in Tokyo—winning two golds, four silvers, and six bronzes, finishing overall in nineteenth place—provided an opportunity for Taiwanese people across the domestic political spectrum to express both pride in the athletes and their preferences for how Taiwan should be recognized abroad.[54]

During the first week of the Tokyo Olympics, the KMT posted a congratulatory message on X (formerly known as Twitter) to the men's archery team for winning a silver medal, not for "#Taiwan" but for "the #ROC," the Republic of China. Unfortunately, for the duration of the Olympics, X was using the hashtag "#ROC" to refer to the Russian Olympic Committee, the team that had been stripped of the right to compete under the name "Russia" due to doping scandals. The company also created a special emoticon to accompany the hashtag, in the shape of the Russian Olympic Committee's emblem. For as long as the emoticon was supported by X, it was retroactively appended to every use of the #ROC hashtag across the entire platform, much to the KMT's consternation. On August 3, the party issued a press release stating, "This has truly caused a complex situation for our compatriots and other relevant parties when tagging #ROC on Twitter [X]; it has also caused confusion on the international stage." It called on President Tsai of the DPP to remonstrate to X.[55] The press release affirmed the KMT's enduring commitment to the Republic of China, the state they founded in 1912, despite its gradual passing into history due to the rise of both the PRC and a distinctively Taiwanese identity.

This tide is even visible for those who come from traditional strongholds of KMT support. For example, the badminton player Lee Yang 李洋 celebrated his Olympic victory in the men's doubles final on July 31, 2021, with a Facebook post that said, "Today, I want to proudly tell everyone again: I am Lee Yang, I am a Kinmenese, I come from Taiwan. We have let the world see Taiwan."[56] Kinmen, an island less than ten kilometers off the coast of Fujian Province near the Chinese city of Xiamen, became part of the ROC at its founding in 1912 and was retained by the KMT when it made its retreat to Taiwan in 1949. It continued to be a frontline of a hot war between the ROC and PRC in the 1950s.

Today, public opinion in Kinmen reflects a generational divide, with older residents often welcoming peaceful engagement with China and younger people like Lee Yang frequently associating the island with an archipelago nation they describe as "Taiwan."[57] Regardless, Taiwan's contested place in the international system limits the vocabulary and symbolism with which people can express their viewpoints. In his post, Lee also included a row of emoticons of the Republic of China flag, which consists of the KMT party emblem set against a red background. There is, after all, no official "Taiwan" flag available for use.

Yet these restrictions also create opportunities for creative and non-traditional expressions of Taiwanese identity. Lee and Wang won their gold medals in a match against China when they hit a shuttlecock that landed right on the service line of the court and the judges deemed it to be in. Almost instantly memes started circulating online, joking that a picture of a badminton court—conveniently green, a color associated with the DPP and Taiwanese sovereignty—could serve as a new Taiwanese national flag. Within days, enterprising manufacturers had produced face masks, T-shirts, and tote bags with a stylized iconography based on the winning play, the intersecting horizontal and vertical white lines of the court borders used to spell out the "T" in Taiwan, the lucky shuttlecock serving as the dot of the "i."[58]

In this symbolic play, Taiwanese people straddle the line between *being* and *becoming*: being citizens of an independent country and announcing themselves as such; and trying to become an independent country, pushing back against arguments that Taiwan is reducible to the ROC or belongs to the PRC. In doing so, they look toward a possible future where they are welcomed into the international community simply as "Taiwan".

NOTES

1. Hale, "Taiwan's Enduring Fascination with Japanese Architecture.".
2. Lee, *Two Trees Make a Forest*, chapter 2.
3. Sugimoto, "Urban Settler Colonialism," 232.
4. Sugimoto, 231, 228.
5. Speidel, "The Administrative and Fiscal Reforms of Liu Ming-ch'uan in Taiwan, 1884–1891."
6. Wu, "Walking in Colonial Taiwan"; Wu and Hsu, "Phantasmagoric Venues from the West to the East," 241.
7. Edmonds, "Aspects of the Taiwanese Landscape in the 20th Century," 2. Edmonds, citing the work of Taiwanese academic Huang Wu-dar 黃武達, notes that "For example the municipality of Taipei grew in area from 4.45 sq km in 1895 to 61.322 sq km by 1935. However, the amount of land vacant in the municipality also grew from about 50 per cent to about 75 per cent of total area and thus the expansion represented planning for future growth of the city."
8. Allen, *Taipei*, 68.
9. Allen, 78.
10. Chang, "Victorian Japan in Taiwan," 1.
11. Barclay, "Peddling Postcards and Selling Empire," 106.
12. Allen, *Taipei*, 129.
13. Chen, "The attempt to integrate the empire: legal perspectives," 271 (citing a statistic from 1942).
14. Cheung, "Taiwan in Time," 13.
15. Zhongshan Hall, "Victory in the War Against Japan and the Retrocession of Taiwan."
16. Yang, "The 228 Massacre in Taipei."
17. Kuo, "Former fugitive designs monument," 15c.
18. For recent English-language work on the memorialization of highly contested, once-suppressed histories in Taiwan, see Chen, "Museums and National History in Conflict"; and Denton, *The Landscape of Historical Memory.*
19. Kang, "From Cairo to the nationalistic geography of China," 48–49, 64.
20. National Museum of Taiwan History, Permanent Exhibition placard titled "Waisheng renkou bili dayu 30% de xiangzhen qu ditu (1965)" 外省人口比例大於30%的鄉鎮區地圖 (1965) [Map of Townships, Villages,

and Districts where the Chinese Mainlander Population Exceeded 30% (1965)].

21. In the November 2022 mayoral elections, the KMT ex-legislator Chiang Wan-an (Wayne Chiang) 蔣萬安, the purported great-grandson of Chiang Kai-shek, was elected the next mayor of Taipei in a three-way race, with 42.3% of the vote. Chen Shih-chung, the former Minister of Health who oversaw the Tsai Ing-wen administration's Covid-19 response, placed second with 31.9% of the vote. "Chiang Wan-an wins Taipei for KMT in tight three-way mayoral race," *Focus Taiwan (CNA English News)*, November 26, 2022.

22. Lien, "Comparing Sources and Patterns of Racial and Ethnic Formation in Taiwan and among Chinese/Taiwanese Americans," 10.

23. National Museum of Taiwan History, Permanent Exhibition placard titled "Map of Townships, Villages, and Districts where the Chinese Mainlander Population Exceeded 30% (1965)."

24. Qingtian 76, "Family and Personal Life"; and Huang, "A Walk on the Mild Side." For more on the construction of faculty housing in what was then known as the Showa-Cho neighborhood of Taipei, see Kuo and Shimizu, "Plan composition and actual conditions of official university residences in former Showa-Cho during the Japanese colonial period in Taiwan."

25. "Da'an Forest Park used to be this way! Taipei residents: I lived here 30 years and only now knew."

26. Archicake architecture firm, *Indistinct Memories, Lost Landscapes* (*Mohu de jiyi, xiaoshi de dijing* 模糊的記憶，消失的地景), Exhibition at Da'an Forest Park, Taipei, Taiwan, October 16–November 15, 2020. Quotation taken from personal photograph by Catherine Chou.

27. Chang, "So close, yet so far away," 403.

28. Chang, 389.

29. Conscription for men was first introduced in Taiwan in 1951 and ranged from two to three years until the early 1990s. As of the writing of this book, plans are being finalized to increase the length of conscription from four months back up to one year, in the face of intensified military harassment from the PRC. "Tsai seeks to finalize conscription plan," *Taipei Times*, December 23, 2022, p. 1.

30. Mao, "Fashioning curriculum reform as identity politics – Taiwan's dilemma of curriculum reform in new millennium," 589.

31. See chapter 3, "How the Kaohsiung Incident Contributed to Taiwan's Democratic Movement" of Jacobs, *The Kaohsiung Incident in Taiwan and Memoirs of a Foreign Big Beard*, 103–111.

32. See Chapter 6, "Dangwai Historiography," in Hsiau, *Politics and Cultural Nativism in 1970s Taiwan: Youth, Narrative, Nationalism.*
33. Bureau of Consular Affairs, ROC (Taiwan), "MOFA [Ministry of Foreign Affairs to release new passport to highlight TAIWAN in January 2021," September 4, 2020; Ko Shu-ling and Charles Snyder, "Chen says the NUC will 'cease'," *Taipei Times*, February 28, 2006, 1.
34. Denton, *The Landscape of Historical Memory*, 13.
35. Wu, "The Black Iron Cage."
36. Indeed, after leaving office in 2000, Lee co-founded the Taiwan Solidarity Union (*Taiwan tuanjie lianmeng*台灣團結聯盟), a party that advocates for the establishment of a Republic of Taiwan. See Jacobs and Liu, "Lee Teng-hui and the Idea of 'Taiwan,'" 390.
37. *Our 1990*; and "Why aren't we angry? The Wild Lily Student Movement," 1:12:28.
38. The rescinded provisions relating to martial law were known as the *Dongyuan kanluan shiqi lingshi tiaokuan*動員戡亂時期臨時條款 [Temporary provisions effective during the period of national mobilization for suppression of the communist rebellion].
39. Chen and Madjar, "Removal of Chiang statue prioritized," 1; and Chen and Chung, "Exhibition to show redesigns for Chiang Kai-shek Memorial Park," 3.
40. Turton, "Notes from Central Taiwan," 8.
41. Chen, Lin, and Yang, "Curriculum and National Identity," 6.
42. Haggerty, "The Troublemaker."
43. For more on the Sunflower Movement, see Wu, "The Black Iron Cage"; Ho, *Challenging Beijing's Mandate of Heaven*; Rowen, "Inside Taiwan's Sunflower Movement"; and Beckershoff, "The Sunflower Movement."
44. See Morris, "A Visual Dialogue of the 2014 Sunflower Movement, 5 Years Later."
45. Rowen, "Inside Taiwan's Sunflower Movement"; and Ho, "The Activist Legacy of Taiwan's Sunflower Movement."
46. For more on the "third wave" parties that emerged from or were invigorated by the Sunflower Movement, see Nachman, "Misalignment between Social Movements and Political Parties in Taiwan's 2016 Election."
47. Wang, "NHK female veteran announcer corrects name of Taiwan's national team."
48. Seven Network Broadcast of Tokyo 2020 Opening Ceremony, July 23, 2021, video clip.

49. Horne and Whannel, *Understanding the Olympics*, 189–191.

50. Taiwan has been a member of the WTO as the "Separate Customs Territory of Taiwan, Penghu, Kinmen, and Matsu" since January 1, 2002.

51. Cady, "Canada Softens on Taiwan, Start of Olympics Assured," A1.

52. Chan, "The 'Two Chinas' Problem and the Olympic Formula," 481.

53. Central Election Commission, "Announcement of the nationwide referendum measures 7 to 16 voting notice," October 24, 2018; and "Announcement of the nationwide referendum measures 7 to 16 voting notice," November 30, 2018.

54. International Olympics Committee, "Tokyo 2020 Medal Table."

55. "Russian Olympic Committee Flag Appearing Next to president Tsai's #ROC Tweet, Tsai Administration Should Convey its Concern," Kuomintang press release, August 3, 2021.

56. Lee Yang, Facebook post, July 31, 2021, 9:24 a.m. The original Mandarin reads: 「我是李洋，我是金門人，我來自台灣⋯⋯我們麟洋讓世界看見了台灣」. See also Chien, "Taiwan's gold medal win over China in badminton raises tensions."

57. Lee, "The Marginalized People of the Borderlands"; and Gerry Shih, "On China's Front Line, Emerging Cold War Haunts Battle-Worn Taiwanese Islands.".

58. Lin Ching-yi, Twitter post, August 12, 2021, 1:55 a.m. Lee, a legislator for the DPP, posted a photo of herself and wrote: "My new face mask! It is a celebration for #TaiwanTeam got the champion of badminton competition of #Olympics!" https://x.com/minorta/status/1425712533722210304

CHAPTER 4

TAIWAN IN THE WORLD

TAIWAN: OUT OF TIME, OUT OF PLACE

In mid-August 2022 at Australia's National Press Club in Canberra, a journalist addressed a question about Taiwan to Xiao Qian, China's ambassador to Australia: "There are twenty-three million people in Taiwan. Don't they get a say in what should happen to their future?" After a digression on Hong Kong, the ambassador replied, unmoved, "The future of Taiwan will be decided by 1.4 billion Chinese people." He added that "my personal understanding is that once Taiwan is united, come back to the motherland, there might be a process for the people in Taiwan to have a correct understanding of China."[1] The exchange was notable less for the hard line expressed by a representative of the People's Republic of China on unification than for the rare recognition in a public forum outside of Taiwan of a Taiwanese subjectivity. The journalist's question suggested a basic truth that is often overlooked: that the Taiwanese should have a right for their voices to be heard and even a right to self-determination.

Xiao's comments at the National Press Club highlights Taiwan's tenuous place in the world and the way Taiwan stands both out of time (suspended perpetually in a radically uncertain future at the inflection point between nationhood and war) and out of place (a state that is unrecognized as a state in the international system). For decades now, Taiwan has been understood less as a place with its own story and agency and more through a rhetorical shorthand as a fault line of geopolitics between the United States and China. Since the Taiwan Strait crises in 1954 and 1958, when Beijing launched a military attempt to take control of the islands of Kinmen and Matsu and the ROC army defended them with the direct support of the United States, Taiwan has existed as a global flashpoint over which war between superpowers might erupt. As China has risen to be the world's second largest economy and a military peer competitor to the United States, Taiwan's status as a flashpoint has only become more pronounced.

In the same month that the Chinese ambassador addressed Australia's national media, Taiwan also received a visit by then Speaker of the United States House of Representatives, Nancy Pelosi. The following day, on August 4, the People's Liberation Army launched seven days of military exercises encircling Taiwan. It fired ballistic missiles over the island and conducted naval and air force exercises simulating an invasion. PLA forces repeatedly crossed the "median line" down the middle of the Taiwan Strait, which had since the 1980s served as a tacit acknowledgment of the two sides' willingness to avoid military conflict. The PLA Air Force continued to conduct flights over the line after the exercises ended. The PLA Navy issued a statement claiming it had been able to compel the US Navy's aircraft carrier, the USS Ronald Reagan, to move away from its position observing the exercises to the east of Taiwan.[2]

In historical terms, the visit by Nancy Pelosi was a high-level one; the last US Speaker of the House to visit Taiwan was Newt Gingrich in 1997. In the context of Beijing's military build-up in the 2020s, however, the Speaker's visit merely served as another pretext for escalating its threats toward Taiwan. While Beijing's military exercises were predictable, they were still a shock to the international system. They triggered statements calling for de-escalation from national capitals around the world, which triggered denunciations from Beijing, followed by the news reporting, policy analysis, and policy decisions responding to each unfolding development. Of such repetitive spirals is Taiwan's status as a flashpoint made.[3]

This intensifying cycle shows not only how Taiwan really is such a flashpoint for war but how Taiwan's very existence is a form of crisis for the international system itself. The "international system" is the name given to the forces of state power and global institutions that emerged after World War II, encompassing both theories of statehood, sovereignty, and territorialization as well as the ways in which such theories are put into practice and mapped onto specific parts of the world. It is a system that contains two contending forces. One is a world shaped by agreed-upon rules and norms, in which there is a functioning structure of nation-states participating as equals in international institutions like the United Nations and also in multilateral agreements. The other is a world shaped by power, in which the international order is wrought by strong states to suit their interests.[4] What is called the "international system" contains both of these forces, and each point toward different global futures: the liberal promise of international law and a rule-based international order, in which states address their shared and conflicting interests through institutions and work together for the overall betterment of humanity, or the cold realist vision of an anarchic system in which states contend for power, territory and hegemony.

China's military exercises toward Taiwan make visible the dark side of the international system. Such actions cast doubt on the idea of China as a responsible member of the international system contributing to the global community through its economic growth and expanding civil society, developments that had so inspired policymakers around the world in the 2000s and 2010s. They point to a future in which China could pursue its national interests, or the ideological fixations of its party-state system, by invading Taiwan and occupying the island against the wishes of the

Taiwanese people—even if this means war with the United States and its allies. China now raises the specter of a naked battle for dominance in Asia and potentially world war.

In this world where China threatens Taiwan with increasingly risky brinkmanship and challenges the stability of the international system, Taiwan itself becomes, to use the self-deprecating phrase used by Taiwanese people, a "ghost island" (*guidao* 鬼島). It is less a real place than a spectral presence. Like the ghosts to which many Taiwanese people make ritual offerings in their everyday lives, Taiwan is a state in the international system that cannot be seen or recognized as such, out of concern that doing so will trigger conflict. It becomes an "issue" or a "problem" in which the prospects for peace or war in the world are continually and simultaneously present. In its current de facto independent condition, Taiwan keeps the international system poised between the possibility of terrible conflict stemming from irredentist territorial claims and the liberal ideal of self-determination, democracy, and progress.

Currently, a coherent national Taiwanese story cannot be told in terms that will be understood within the international system, according to which Taiwan has no territory or history, neither having entered nor left this system under its name. This national story has only ever been the unfulfilled aspiration of Taiwanese people. These circumstances are what made the question from the Australian journalist to the Chinese ambassador about the fate of 23 million people so notable. In that moment, Taiwan was not merely a scapegoat or a problem. Instead, the Taiwanese briefly took on a corporeal presence in global public discourse, becoming recognized as real people with interests and preferences of their own.

National governments have developed elaborate policy formulations and arcane diplomatic language to manage the contradictions revealed by Taiwan's existence. Like a ghost, Taiwan is an unspoken presence around which normal international life proceeds, sometimes tolerated, sometimes feared, often a source of anxiety, and even occasionally welcomed but not officially recognized. Foreign governments have "representatives"—not ambassadors—in Taipei, and their embassies are referred to as "Offices" or "Institutes," for example, the American Institute in Taiwan, the Australian Office, or the Canadian Trade Office in Taipei. Governments such as the US, Canada, and Australia have "one China" policies that "recognize" the People's Republic of China as a state, while only "acknowledge[ing]" Beijing's position that Taiwan is a province of China.[5] The governments that use these policy mechanisms are like mediums in the international system's spirit world speaking to Taiwan through esoteric incantations. When legislators from the US Congress or the European Parliament visit Taiwan, they cross over into this world, as if seeing for the first time a world with different, more compelling, moral certainties than the compromises made by the "real world" in dealing with Taiwan. Delegations often frame their visits in terms of discovery or wonder at Taiwan's achievements as a democracy and powerhouse economy.

This creates a disjuncture between the way that Taiwanese people experience their lives and the way that Taiwan exists in and out of the international system. The seemingly indifferent attitude of Taiwanese people to Beijing's military threats, which so confuses international observers, can be understood as an expression of this disjuncture. Closed off by design to Taiwanese perspectives, the international system struggles to grasp the experience of a people who simply have no choice but to live with the threatening presence of their huge neighbor and whose everyday life is a form of resistance to relentless efforts to define their identity on their behalf.[6]

The Republic of China (ROC): From Center to Margin and Back

The fact that Taiwanese today still live under a state—the Republic of China—that has moved from the center of the post–World War II international system to its margins and now, in destabilizing and uncertain fashion, back to the center of its geopolitics, reinforces the contradictions and absurdities of life as a Taiwanese person. For four years, between

1945 and 1949, Taiwan was part of a cross-Strait "one China" known as
the Republic of China. Then, for four decades after its loss in the Chinese
Civil War and the founding of the People's Republic of China in 1949,
the KMT governed Taiwan as a single-party authoritarian state, using
the island and its people to claim that the Republic of China was still the
legitimate government of "all of China." As Taiwan democratized and
people who identified themselves as Taiwanese were allowed into the
upper echelons of government, the ROC apparatus remained in place,
serving as both the state that administered the island and—when not
edged out by the PRC—as the entity under which the people living on
the island could engage in formal diplomatic relations. The ROC flag—
designed for a country that did not include Taiwan in its official territory
or self-conception at its founding in 1911—has today become, in various
contexts, a symbol of Taiwanese identity. As of the writing of this book,
this second version of the ROC is recognized only by twelve countries
plus the Vatican and has no seat at the United Nations. Even this tenuous
hold, however, allows Taiwanese access to some international-level
events and exchanges, such as inaugurations and ambassadorial get-
togethers where other diplomats are present. These avenues may yet be
cut off if the number of countries recognizing the ROC ever reaches zero.

Ironically, the ROC of which Taiwan was a part, from 1945 to 1949,
was at the center of the post–World War II international system and the
hope it offered for a better world. The Republic was an Allied Power.
Its scholars and diplomats, including Ching-lin Hsia 夏晋麟 and Kuo
Tai-chi 郭泰祺, participated in the negotiations for the establishment
of the United Nations in 1946 and the composition of the UN Charter.
References to the Republic of China remain in the UN Charter like an
archaeological artefact of a different era. Article 110 states that: "The
present Charter shall come into force upon the deposit of ratifications by
the Republic of China, France, the Union of Soviet Socialist Republics, the
United Kingdom of Great Britain and Northern Ireland, and the United
States of America, and by a majority of the other signatory states." Article
23 still states: "The Security Council shall consist of fifteen Members of

the United Nations. The Republic of China, France, the Union of Soviet Socialist Republics, the United Kingdom of Great Britain and Northern Ireland, and the United States of America shall be permanent members of the Security Council."[7]

The fate of the ROC also soon helped to expose the fragility of the UN's liberal international promise. The Korean War, the nascent Cold War, and the Taiwan Strait crises of the 1950s revealed an international system divided by regional conflict and emerging global blocs, over which new risks of global catastrophe loomed in the nuclear age. As the ROC had animated the progressive hopes of the international system at its inception, it soon fed its mirror image of state rivalry, crisis, and war. The Soviet bloc recognized the government of PRC in Beijing from its founding in 1949. In the 1960s and 1970s, many other countries also switched recognition from the ROC to the PRC. As the PRC increased in legitimacy and economic might, it showed how the development of an international system built on the liberal values of the equality of states and the principle of self-determination had from the outset compromised with state power and state ideology, as it acted to prevent people in Taiwan from forming a new internationally recognized nation that could facilitate their entrance into this same system. The ROC can seem like a curio, its fragments scattered everywhere about the international system and generating confusion about Taiwan's identity. But the ROC is also a mechanism through which the world is held in balance between competing forces. So long as the ROC exists in some form in Taiwan, then Taiwan has neither vanished through forced unification with the PRC nor emerged into the world as a sovereign Taiwanese nation-state.

For these reasons, people in Taiwan are divided on whether to retain or dismantle the ROC. Some argue for its legitimacy. After all, it has been the official government of Taiwan for more than three-quarters of a century. For others, the ROC has already been functionally reduced to the island and people of Taiwan. Others see it as an obstacle to the establishment of a truly sovereign Taiwanese state.

Since democratization, Taiwan's various governments have emphasized the name and existence of ROC to greater or lesser degrees, with their strategies shaped by domestic and partisan factors. Typically, the KMT leans into its party's history as the founder of the ROC, while the DPP speaks to two audiences: its domestic base that has little interest in ROC identity and an international audience for which Taiwan's identity politics are a metric of cross-Strait tension and for whom acknowledgments of the ROC are necessary. In her speeches, heard by both domestic and international audiences, President Tsai Ing-wen of the DPP has acknowledged this dilemma by describing her role as the "president of the Republic of China (Taiwan)." In her address on October 10, 2021, the National Day of the ROC, President Tsai stated that "amid this evolving global landscape, the Republic of China today finds itself in a situation that is more complex and fluid than at any other point in the past seventy-two years. Every step we take will influence our world's future direction, and our world's future direction will likewise affect the future of Taiwan itself."[8] Although it was the 110th National Day, Tsai kept her focus on the seventy-two years since 1949, when the fates of the ROC and Taiwan merged. Tsai's careful nomenclature gestured to both the ROC's role in shaping and being shaped by the postwar order as well as a parallel, alternative future of this system that includes rather than excludes Taiwan.

TAIWAN IN THE WORLD

Taiwan is thus a spectral presence that reveals the history and contradictions of the postwar international order. For Beijing, however, even this spectral presence is too much to countenance. It claims that Taiwan is a province of the PRC. It repeatedly challenges attempts by states, nongovernmental organizations, and individual people to act and speak in ways that confer the trappings of real statehood upon Taiwan and national identity on Taiwanese people. Beijing polices language and symbolism around the world about Taiwan obsessively, remonstrating against the display of the ROC flag, meetings with national-level Taiwanese ministers, and countless other minor infractions to its worldview. In rote formulations, the PRC Ministry of Foreign Affairs asserts, "First, there is only one China in the world. The government of the People's Republic of China is the sole legal government representing the whole of China. The Taiwan region is an inalienable part of the Chinese territory." It adds, "A total of 180 countries, including the US, have established diplomatic relations with China on the basis of the one China principle," even though the United States, in common with many states, adheres to its own "one China *policy*" (emphasis added) that acknowledges, but does not recognize, the PRC claim to Taiwan.[9] Beijing uses its international influence to marginalize Taiwan in the world in an obdurate refusal to acknowledge the island's history and identity. For Beijing, keeping Taiwan's status anomalous and irregular has always been an expression of nothing less than its capacity to shape the world's realities through ideologically directed state power. Beijing insists that there is only a single reality—that Taiwan is a part of China—and seeks to make the world see it in the same way.

In the middle of the twentieth century, Beijing committed to this worldview through a policy of "liberation" of Taiwan through military force. In the emerging Cold War divide, the ROC signed the Sino-American Mutual Defense Treaty, a formal military alliance that placed Taiwan on the US side against the communist world. Taiwan became "Free China," all while the KMT maintained one of the longest military rules in modern history, oftentimes brutally suppressing dissent against its regime and aspirations toward Taiwanese identity, nationhood, and sovereignty. During the Second Taiwan Strait Crisis in 1958, the PLA and ROC military clashed over the island of Dongding, with the PLA's Soviet MiG-15 and MiG-17 jets engaging the ROC's US F-86s in dogfights across the Taiwan Strait. With no progress for the PLA, a ceasefire was declared in October 1958 and the strange ritual of alternate-day shelling of the island of Kinmen (Quemoy) began. Giant speakers were set up to broadcast propaganda messages in each direction, and balloons carrying propaganda leaflets were regularly floated across by both sides.

The turning point came in the 1970s when the Mao period gave way to the era of Reform and Opening Up, just as Taipei was losing international recognition as the ROC. Beijing and Washington underwent a decade of rapprochement under the realpolitik of successive US administrations, secretly in the late 1960s, publicly in 1972 with Nixon's visit, until diplomatic relations were established in 1979. Taiwan was still under one-party rule by the KMT when the National People's Congress in Beijing issued the "Letter to Taiwan Compatriots" in 1979. This letter identified party-to-party negotiations between the CCP and the KMT as the pathway toward the goal of Beijing called "reunification." It was a significant shift from the previous failed military "liberation" policy.[10] In 1981, Beijing's approach to unification was codified into the "one country, two systems" formula as part of "Nine Principles" put forward by Marshal Ye Jianying 葉劍英, a veteran of the Chinese Civil War. This stance has since become a nonnegotiable position for Beijing regarding Taiwan, although "one country, two systems" has little to no support from the KMT, the DPP, or the Taiwanese people.

In the Xi Jinping era, Taiwan has come to occupy a central position in the CCP's policies and ideologies. In the utopian vision of its current rhetoric, the unification of Taiwan with the is portrayed as essential to China's "Great Rejuvenation." According to the contradictions of the CCP's Marxist scientism, unification is both an inevitable outcome in accordance with history's immutable laws and an imperiled future that the party must struggle to achieve against revisionist forces.

In 2022, Beijing's Taiwan Affairs Office released a white paper, the third one after 1993 and 2000, that further codified its Taiwan ideology: Taiwan is part of China in terms of both history and international law and must be unified with the People's Republic. Beijing hopes that this will happen peacefully, but separatists and foreign forces are conspiring to prevent it and so military action might be required.[11] In articulating its position,

Beijing often mobilizes the founding liberal principles of the international system of sovereignty, territorial integrity, and institutionalization to justify its claim, arguing that the PRC is the successor state to the ROC under international law. In the 2022 Taiwan white paper, Beijing places great emphasis on UN Resolution 2758, which granted to the PRC entry to the UN, including a seat on the Security Council, as the legitimate government of China. However, the resolution text excludes the "representatives of Chiang Kai-shek" and does not mention Taiwan or to its sovereignty.[12] Likewise, Beijing also works to blur the distinction between "one China" policies of other governments such as those of the United States and Australia, and its own "one China" principle. It often claims that these countries already adhere to Beijing's unambiguous "one China principle" and then tendentiously asserts that these countries are breaching their own diplomatic commitments.

The language of officials in China's party-state system is fine-tuned to navigate this recondite ideological and policy system. These officials generate furious, inflammatory rhetoric and uncompromising demands to affirm Beijing's worldview on Taiwan. Beijing's ideological fixations are intrinsically contradictory. It simultaneously seeks to efface the ROC and yet portrays any moves by Taiwanese actors to reduce the role or presence of the ROC as provocation. The pursuit of self-determination by the Taiwanese through democracy means that they are refusing to move in the historical direction that the CCP believes they should. The end of the authoritarian era in Taiwan and the institutionalization of free and fair elections have allowed Taiwanese to openly discuss their history, demography, and identities, challenging the notion that Taiwan has been part of China since ancient times and only "split" in 1949. Democratization has so altered Taiwan that the ROC army—which arrived in Taiwan at the end of World War II and originally served the goal of the KMT party-state to "retake the mainland"—is now a nationalized institution tasked with protecting a polity whose inhabitants overwhelmingly reject "unification with the mainland." The CCP's threat to launch an invasion of Taiwan to achieve its goals is an admission that its theoretical foundations regarding Taiwan are flawed. In a system that sees itself as scientifically correct under Marxist theory, Taiwan's incorrect identity and sovereignty must be explained. This is done by externalizing blame onto "secessionists" and the conspiratorial "foreign forces" that support Taiwan's continued sovereignty.

In practice, the nature of China's party-state system makes a self-critical reassessment impossible. Beijing is thus locked into a cycle of tactical escalation, continuously increasing military and diplomatic pressure on Taiwan, which only strengthens Taiwanese resolve, leading Beijing to conclude that even more pressure is needed. The support of the US and other countries for Taiwan through visits by elected representatives, bilateral agreements, weapons sales, and naval transits through the Taiwan Strait fuels Beijing's perception of foreign forces colluding with Taiwanese separatists, which in turn motivates escalation.

The PRC is becoming powerful enough that its assertion of its territorial claim over Taiwan, through growing military and diplomatic pressure, is reshaping the international system. The increasing capacity of the PRC to pursue its irredentist territorial claims is transforming the international system. The competing impetuses of liberal internationalism and anarchism are giving way to an open contest for power, with China on one side, the US and its allies on another, and Taiwan as the focal point of this struggle.[13] However much lip service is paid to the postwar liberal ideals of peace, progress, and international order, these ideals are being tested by an emerging great power that seeks to redraw its national boundaries by force. In this way, the Taiwan Strait records the failures of the postwar international system to fully reconcile its contradictions since its inception. This can only be a fearful portent, and the ROC armed forces, as well as the US and other national militaries, devote significant resources to preparing for a scenario where Beijing invades and occupies Taiwan. The People's Liberation Army focuses its planning, training, and procurement on such action, while the PRC party-state has already demonstrated its willingness to use the unconstrained power of the state against the challenges it identifies, from Uyghur "reeducation" in Xinjiang, to harsh lockdowns to suppress the COVID-19 virus, to imprisoning political dissidents in Hong Kong, to marginalizing and restricting Taiwan.

Assessing these forces is made more difficult because Taiwan's presence both outside the international system and at the center of its contradictions means that seeking to know and understand it is, by definition, a subversive practice. For global civil society, including policy analysis, media reporting, and at the level of the everyday, developing an analysis or account of Taiwan requires standing outside the rules of the international system, as the Taiwanese themselves do, and speaking directly about Taiwan as a society, a state, and even a nation. However, due to Beijing's claims, Taiwan is sublimated into different disguises rather than addressed squarely, that is, spoken *about* rather than spoken *to*. Taiwan is misrepresented, misnamed, and described as a moral and geopolitical dilemma for the world, while the rich complexity of Taiwan's story and the voices of the Taiwanese people themselves struggle to be heard.

For example, analyses of cross-strait relations in the media and by policy think tanks have a distinctive focus on timelines for "unification." These countdowns function as a doomsday clock, ticking down to when China attacks Taiwan and the United States intervenes and is drawn into a war directly with China. Kevin Rudd, former Australian prime minister, has said that Xi Jinping is determined to achieve unification by the late 2020s or early 2030s and that "the real risk of war will escalate markedly" in this period. According to Rudd, "Xi Jinping, for the first time, has set an effective deadline for Taiwan's return no later than the centenary of the People's Republic of China in 2049."[14] What the Taiwanese want is ignored in this discourse, even though what they want —and do not want—is clear. Furthermore, given the opaque nature of the PRC system, the ever-changing balance of power in the Taiwan Strait, and China's unpredictable domestic social and economic conditions, it is ultimately unknowable whether China's leadership has a firm deadline for invasion and unification. China has never made such a bald declaration but instead acts tactically and opportunistically, using its own version of strategic ambiguity to maximize its leverage over policy on Taiwan. However, the focus on ascribing specific timelines for unification amid such uncertainties serves to highlight how Taiwan activates the anxieties and contradictions of the international system, rather than providing a deterministic prediction of an invasion.

Similarly, the field of international relations frequently engages in discussions about the prospects of war "over Taiwan" and the choices that the US and its allies would face. Recommendations are offered to avert a crisis, either by "resum[ing] military activities around Taiwan... including transits through the Taiwan Strait and operations in international waters that China claims as its own"[15] or by deploying American diplomatic power to coax China and Taiwan toward a "peaceful" resolution of their dispute.[16] Taiwanese subjectivity is necessarily discounted in such prescriptions because they are aimed instead at preserving or renegotiating the post–World War II ideal of *Pax Americana*.

TAIWANESE IN THE WORLD

Despite the geopolitical forces in play, it is Taiwanese subjectivity that continues to change the cross-Strait story time and again, standing against the assumed outcome of "unification." It is the Taiwanese desire for democracy and for the recognition by the global community that has so far put off unification. In response, the Chinese government targets this subjectivity in myriad major and minor ways, using its power and influence to normalize its position on the marginalization and even erasure of Taiwanese people and organizations. It is an increasingly monomaniacal attempt to turn the tide of history in the direction Taiwanese people do not wish to go in.

This activity has shaped the representation of Taiwan in unlikely settings. In the northern Australian city of Rockhampton, famous for its cattle farming, there is an annual festival called Beef Week. In 2018, the event organizers commissioned full-sized cattle sculptures and invited local school children to paint national flags representing their cultural heritage onto them. When two Taiwanese Australian children painted the flag of the ROC, the city council ordered workers to paint over their flags to accord with what they argued was the concept of "one China."[17] That same year, international airlines in the US and elsewhere altered their booking websites to remove singular references to Taiwan and replace them with "Taiwan, China," explicitly to accommodate a request by the Civil Aviation Authority of China because the airlines wanted to keep their access to the China air travel market.[18] The following year, the website of the World Mobile Congress (a mobile phone industry event in Barcelona, Spain, attended by 60,000 participants) required Taiwanese to register themselves as hailing from "Taiwan, Province of China," with event organizers declining entreaties to change this designation. Even though Taiwan is central to technology supply chains in the mobile phone industry, Taiwan government officials were compelled to withdraw their attendance.[19] In 2020, BirdLife International, the United Kingdom-based conservation organization, which works with local and national groups around the world to protect birds, expelled the Taiwan-based Chinese Wild Bird Federation (CWBF) after it refused a request to change its name and sign a pledge to not promote or advocate for Taiwan independence. BirdLife International issued a demand that the CWBF "Cease (in any and all languages)...to use the expression 'Republic of China' and/or other expressions or symbols suggesting adherence to the independence position of Chinese Taiwan" and "[f]ormally commit...not to advocate or promote in any other way the independence of Chinese Taiwan or the legitimacy of the 'Republic of China'."[20]

Sometimes, Taiwan wins these contests, or else they end in a draw. In 2020, the website of Australia's national postal service, Australia Post, showed Taiwan along with Hong Kong and Macao as regions of the PRC but revised the listing after the intervention of the Australian government. Similarly, the visa registration website of the 2022 FIFA

World Cup in Qatar listed Taiwan as "Taiwan, Province of China" but dropped the provincial designation after pressure from Tsai Ing-wen's government. Counterpressure from China, however, led to a second change of the name to "Chinese Taipei."[21]

These and innumerable other actions to erase Taiwan and the Taiwanese people, either explicitly at the behest of Chinese government officials or preemptively in response to often unnamed and undefined risk calculations, run in parallel to the arcane diplomatic formulations used by national governments to work around Taiwan's lack of formal statehood. But unlike those policy instruments, the infractions against Taiwan's representation within global civil society are experienced in subjective and often moral terms. Each exclusion or redefinition of Taiwan as a PRC province by an organization or corporate entity is an indignity inflicted upon the Taiwanese people. These nongovernmental actors are, seemingly, choosing to show that the people of Taiwan are unworthy of proper representation in the world. In doing so, they mimic the intense anxiety and hyperbole that Chinese government displays when speaking about Taiwan. BirdLife International, for example, claimed that the use of the "'Republic of China' in the CWBF's name, presentation, and communication poses a serious risk to [our organization and its] mission, and compromises and prejudices its interests and those of the BirdLife Partnership." For an organization committed to protecting animal species that know no national borders, taking the side of China on Taiwan's status can end up seeming both ludicrous and bizarre, and such actions often merely draw more attention to the island's incongruous position. After its ejection, the CWBF decided to change its name in English to the Taiwan Wild Bird Federation (TWBF), "to avoid international confusion and allow us to expand ties with other groups in promoting the important work of global conservation."[22]

Within this context, the 2022 visit to Taiwan by then House Speaker Nancy Pelosi served to validate Taiwan's importance as a de facto state and ally. It was also, of course, a demonstration of American political and military power. By contrast, a question by an Australian journalist to the Chinese ambassador about the rights of the Taiwanese to decide their own future offered a more authentic moral refutation of Taiwan's erasure by global forces. It was one that went to the core of the liberal promises of self-determination offered after World War II and showed how febrile global debates about Taiwan can be. But this is a very real question. Will the people of Taiwan in fact be able to decide their own future? What will it mean if they cannot do so? The question becomes not only whether Taiwan is condemned to lose even its spectral presence in the international system but also whether that system will acquiesce to the reality of a "Taiwan province." Will Taiwan have no future and, in being subjected to "unification" at Beijing's insistence, have no history or past either?

Were Taiwan to fall under the authority of Beijing, Taiwan's indigenous history and its history of Japanese colonization, martial law, and democracy will be used by China's party-state system to justify a violent remaking of Taiwanese subjectivity, so that Taiwanese will think of themselves as only ever having belonged to China. In this possible future, Taiwan—as a place with more than a century of post-imperial aspirations for identity, nationhood, democracy, and modernity—becomes a place with the wrong past, one that needs to be erased for it to fulfill its role as a symbol of the CCP's "Great Rejuvenation of the Chinese Nation." As Ambassador Xiao stated to the Australian media, the people of Taiwan would need to be "reeducated" to forget their history and relearn a new one, as they were required once to do before under the authoritarian rule of another authoritarian Chinese party-state.

Of course, as is apparent in other contested territories on China's borderlands, Taiwan's "incorrect" history will also always be needed by the party-state to validate unification. The people of Taiwan will be required to forget that they are Taiwanese but simultaneously always be reminded of this identity by a state that needs to show them as defeated and ensconced within Chinese borders to legitimize the CCP's narrative of a reunited and rejuvenated nation. For the rest of the world, this vision of the future is one of acute and prolonged crisis, involving possibly millions of refugees, internment camps, and mass political imprisonment. Beijing's vision of "Great Rejuvenation" is only rendered meaningful in an international system that acknowledges it, and this means an insistence that the whole world forgets Taiwan and the Taiwanese story in favor of one about "rightful" reunification.

Such a future makes telling the Taiwanese story today even more urgent, given the sense of contingency. Taiwan's journey of imperfect progress from authoritarianism to democracy is inspiring, even though it has yet to be fully validated by recognition as a state in the international system, and this gives it a melancholy optimism. The people of Taiwan, simultaneously outside and at the center of this system, have built a democratic society through struggle and hope, with an atypical experience of state-building and nationhood that holds both moral and existential consequences for the postwar international system. Studying Taiwan and conveying its history and present not only validates and preserves Taiwanese identity in the face of Beijing's military threat, but doing so also creates the very material of Taiwanese national consciousness that the PRC party-state points to as the reason for needing to intervene via military invasion. The more often Taiwan's story is told, the greater the force the PRC will attribute to the "separatists" and "foreign forces" it claims are working to prevent China's rise. Taiwanese identity activates contradictory impulses in a cyclical and, so far, seemingly unresolvable way.

More than ever in the Xi era, as the PRC aggressively asserts its territorial claim over Taiwan, simply observing and commenting upon Taiwan's place in the world may feel insufficient to those who study it. As a subject of inquiry, Taiwan necessarily weakens the distinction between disinterested scholarly knowledge and activism. Instead, the threat of cross-Strait annexation requires confronting what a vast global political and institutional project it would be to abandon and forget Taiwan and its people, who would in all likelihood then be subject to "reeducation," forced exile, and prison or labor camps. The mechanics of disciplining 23 million people who have lived in a democratic, functionally independent polity will roil the politics and rupture the relationships of communities around the world far beyond Taiwan.

Notes

1. National Press Club of Australia, "HE Xiao Qian, Ambassador of the People's Republic of China, Address to the NPC"; and Tillett, "China plans re-education once 'Taiwan is unified.'"
2. "The PLA targets pushing back the Reagan from eastern Taiwan."
3. Australian Government Department of Foreign Affairs and Trade, "U.S.-Australia-Japan Trilateral Strategic Dialogue."
4. Eckert. "Constructing States."
5. Drun, "One China, Multiple Interpretations."
6. Wang and Cheng, "Taiwan Residents Largely Calm in the Face of Chinese Anger." .
7. United Nations, *Charter of the United Nations and statute of the International Court of Justice.*
8. Tsai, "President Tsai delivers 2021 National Day Address."
9. Ministry of Foreign Affairs of the People's Republic of China, "Statement by the Ministry of Foreign Affairs of the People's Republic of China."
10. Standing Committee of the National People's Congress of the People's Republic of China, "Open Letter to Taiwan Compatriots (January 1, 1979).
11. Central Government of the People's Republic of China, "The Taiwan Question and the Work of China's Reunification in the New Era.".
12. Drun and Glaser, *The Distortion of UN Resolution 2758 and Limits on Taiwan's Access to the United Nations.*
13. In international relations, the term "anarchy" is often used to describe the "absence of common authority (office of rule) or the absence of a common ruler...". See Lechner, "Anarchy in International Relations."
14. Rudd, "How to Avoid a Crisis over Taiwan."
15. "Target: Taiwan; America and China," 9.
16. Swaine, Lee, and Odell, "A New Direction."
17. Robinson and Terzon, "Taiwan flag design painted over by council ahead of beef industry Event."
18. Bryan, "Taiwan: How Airlines Are Being Dragged into China's Bitter Dispute over the Island's Sovereignty."
19. "Taiwan protests MWC's labelling of Taiwan as Part of China."
20. "Taiwan's Bird Conservation Group Expelled from BirdLife International."

21. Blanchard, "Taiwan Accuses China of bullying over World Cup name change."

22. Taiwan Wild Bird Federation, "Statement on Taiwan Wild Bird Federation Name Change and Clarifications on Removal from BirdLife International," September 24, 2020.

Epilogue

Taiwanese people live in a peculiar state of freedom. The activists of the 1970s through the early 1990s successfully achieved democratization against the ROC, a brutal, autocratic regime that escaped to Taiwan and attempted to use it as a base to reconquer China. However, even with democratization and the collapse of the ROC's claims to being the true China, there is still no pathway for Taiwan into the community of nations. The CCP has demonstrated some willingness to allow Taiwanese people more access to international space when the KMT wins elections, but it views DPP administrations as de facto illegitimate. Over the past decade, the CCP has employed increasingly sophisticated tactics to flood the Taiwanese information environment with fake social media accounts, deepfakes, conspiracy theories, and manufactured "news" stories. These efforts are intended to diminish Taiwanese confidence in democracy and the competence of duly elected officials.[1] Democracy itself, with its requirement that power be able to change across party lines, is what the PRC demands as the sacrifice for reopened and ostensibly friendlier cross-Strait relations. Thus, Taiwanese people today—including the two generations "born independent" after the lifting of martial law—exist in a geopolitical purgatory, threatened with colonization by yet another authoritarian Chinese party-state, this time, one that is based in Beijing.

The critical question structuring modern Taiwanese life is what it means to flourish in the face of an existential threat, while also dealing with the limitations of a citizenship unrecognized by global institutions, national governments, website drop-down menus, academic publications, and ordinary people worldwide. Preparing to defend against military invasion and countering daily instances of Chinese economic and geopolitical pressure drains Taiwanese resources. This includes tax dollars diverted to buy upgraded weapons, time spent by young men on conscription, the search for ad hoc ways to mimic formal international relations, and the toll of being misidentified, mislabeled, and misunderstood due to one's place of birth and upbringing. Both the external threat of takeover and the domestic cleavages over how to manage the relationship with this powerful neighbor take time and energy away from quality-of-life issues and inhibit long-term vision about how to make Taiwanese society more livable and just for its people. Additional steps toward reforming the ROC system to better match contemporary Taiwan's preferences and needs—whether constitutional, bureaucratic, or political in nature—risk arousing not only domestic opposition from the "deep blue" faction of the KMT but also warnings from the PRC and criticism from world leaders often primed to see Taiwan as a troublemaker. This is the cost of Chinese ethnonationalism—a regionally and globally destabilizing phenomenon that also constrains Taiwanese life across multiple axes in the present, even though an invasion may never come to pass.

"GHOST ISLAND" AND THE "MANGO STRIPS OF DOOM"

Taiwan has been under the shadow of military invasion for more than seventy years, even as the government and people have radically changed in composition, identity, and aspirations for their place in the international order. Having perhaps encountered Taiwan only in headline news, visitors will sometimes marvel that its citizens seem remarkably unconcerned about war or are outright dismissive of the possibility that it will happen. The impact of living under an ever-present but not fully activated threat, however, reveals itself more subtly, in the way that Taiwanese people characterize themselves and their homeland, and in the aggravation of social and economic issues that may undermine Taiwanese prosperity in the long run. In *bentu* ("local") art and commentary, Taiwan is often characterized as a "ghost island," a term meant to convey the "self-doubt and self-mockery" that accompanies life on an "invisible ghost country not officially recognized by the United Nations," as Chia-rong Wu writes.[2] According to Yao-tai Li and Yunya Song, young Taiwanese deploy the term "ghost island" both in a "self-mocking" and "self-assertive way," with a "mixture of grudge, helplessness, pessimism, hope and pride" in their simultaneously marginalized and free status.[3] In a study of Chinese disinformation and misinformation in Taiwanese online spaces, Ho-Chun Herbert Chang and his colleagues examine the circulation of a "ghost island" meme on the online blackboard system Professional Technology Temple (PTT).[4] They conclude that what was originally a "self-deprecating criticism," pointing to local concerns about "opportunity loss, economic stagnation, and government corruption," was also successfully deployed by Chinese users during the 2018 midterm elections "to agitate feelings of emptiness and pessimism towards Taiwan's… future."[5] The phrase is so widely used that even the Taiwanese version of the online dating site OkCupid included the following question for users to answer on their profile: "Do you feel that Taiwan is a ghost island for young people?"[6]

During the 2020 campaign, when the DPP incumbent Tsai Ing-wen's reelection seemed in doubt, young people began speaking of the "sense of the nation's impending doom" using a term called *wangguogan* 亡國感, a phonetic play on the popular snack dried mango strips (*manguogan* 芒果乾 in Mandarin).[7] Sociologist Ming-sho Ho explains that this term referred "to an existential anxiety that Taiwanese might have to forfeit their cherished freedom and lifestyle, should voters choose a presidential candidate"—in this case, the KMT's Han Kuo-yu—"who was perceived to accommodate the PRC's territorial claim over the island."[8] Here, the "doomed nation" being referred to by young people was Taiwan, not the ROC. It is Taiwan, not the ROC, that the PRC demands must accept integration into the PRC, under, at best, a "one country, two systems" arrangement that in the case of Hong Kong has been rapidly collapsed into "one country, less than two systems." The late Arif Dirlik noted that Taiwan is a place where "life is under constant threat of disappearance into the economic, cultural, and possibly, political folds of its powerful mainland counterpart."[9]

This feeling of uncertainty and disquietude about Taiwan's prospects and those of its people manifests itself in several ways: a record-low birth rate, emigration and brain drain, and tendencies toward inwardness and parochialism that make it difficult to globalize along the limited channels available to Taiwanese.

MAKING NEW TAIWANESE

Even as Taiwanese identity has reached new heights—in 2021, National Chengchi University's annual survey stated that 63.3% of respondents self-identified as Taiwanese and another 31.4% as both Taiwanese and Chinese—it has proven difficult to produce new Taiwanese people in the twenty-first century.[10] As an identity that does not correspond to a recognized nation-state and that, due to its origins in dissidence and opposition, has historically been a chosen one, declared rather than only assumed, Taiwaneseness is not necessarily a quality that everyone who is born in Taiwan, lives there, or holds ROC citizenship possesses. Taiwanese people are not simply born; they also have to be inculcated to see themselves as such in a geopolitical environment that both denies and attacks the existence of this identity. Those who describe themselves as Taiwanese also take it upon themselves, in discourse and policy, to try to ascertain who is sufficiently committed to Taiwanese identity— and is therefore worthy of claiming it—and those who are not.

Taiwan has one of the lowest birth rates in the world, at just 7.39 per one thousand people.[11] In 2020, the population dropped as deaths surpassed births, 173,156 to 165,249.[12] Already Taiwan, like South Korea and Japan, is classified as an "aged" society, with more than fourteen percent of the population aged sixty-five or older.[13] The academic literature and reporting on this phenomenon attribute it to multiple factors: relatively low salaries that have not risen at the same pace as in other Asian countries, increases in property prices that have outpaced salary growth, decreased marriage rates, the stigma against out-of-wedlock parenthood, legal restrictions on single women and single-sex couples accessing reproductive technology, and anxiety about bringing children up on a "ghost island." The National Development Council of the ROC estimates that by 2028 Taiwan will be demographically underwater, with the working-age population accounting for less than two-thirds of the total.[14]

Even as Taiwanese society has partially moved toward civic under-standing of identity, countervailing and contradictory notions about the importance of "Chinese" ethnicity remain both popularly and legally enshrined. For the second half of the twentieth century, Taiwan was administered by the elite faction of a minority population, defined according to their rejection of the island as a homeland and their embod-iment of an ostensibly authentic and idealized Chinese identity. Despite this, many *waishengren* intermarried with *benshengren* and indigenous Taiwanese and opted to remain in Taiwan rather than migrate again to another country or later, when the option became available, to "return" to what was now the PRC. Transitioning toward democracy required assuaging their anxieties about majority reprisal and their displacement from a place of political privilege. As historian Dominic Meng-hsuan Yang writes, "the suffering and social dislocation produced by the Nationalist collapse in 1949 cannot negate the…duality [in] first-generation *waishen-gren*: both as displaced refugees from a brutal civil war and overbearing colonizers to the semi-Japanized islanders."[15]

To help manage fears of ethnic tension in a period of political change, Lee Tung-hui, a *benshengren* technocrat who improbably rose to the vice presidency and then presidency in the waning days of one-party KMT rule, popularized the concept of the "new Taiwanese" (*xin Taiwanren* 新台灣人).[16] In this framework, elaborated in scholarship and public service announcements alike, modern Taiwanese society was characterized as a mixture of five "ethnic groups" with equal claims to belonging: indigenous Taiwanese, *waishengren*, Hakka-speakers, Hokkien Taiwanese-speakers, and so-called "new immigrants."[17] This was a "multiethnic" framework, however, that collapsed more than a dozen indigenous tribes with different ancestral languages and settlement practices into a single category. It was a "multiethnic" framework in which three out of five categories— the numerical majority—consisted of people who traced their ancestry to China and who were collectively described as Han 漢人 or Hua 華人 in other contexts. Moreover, although they were not overtly racialized, "new immigrants" overwhelmingly consisted of "marriage migrants" who were often of ethnic Chinese origin as well, and who were also expected to take on the social identities of their new husbands.[18] Taiwan thus became an officially "multiethnic" society without welcoming a significant number of new migrants, at a time when KMT educational policies were succeeding in eroding the very multilingualism that was the basis for designating indigenous Taiwanese, *waishengren*, and Hakka-, and Hokkien-speakers, as different "ethnic groups" to begin with.

ROC law enshrined ethnicity and descent as the basis for nationality and civic rights in post-1945 Taiwan. Yet even as more Taiwanese began rejecting the idea that theirs was or ought to be a Chinese society or nation, the difficulty of reforming core components of the ROC system, suspicion of "Chinese" migrants, *and* entrenched discrimination against indigenous Taiwanese and non-Han minorities, have worked against a more expansive conception of Taiwanese identity. As yet, there is no official Taiwanese nationality or citizenship, only an ROC one. ROC nationality law—*jus sanguinis* in nature—is largely unchanged from the original 1929 version, devised before it was possible to know that Taiwan would become part of the ROC. According to Article Two of the Nationality Act, "any person shall have the nationality of the ROC [whose] father or mother was a national when he or she was born."[19] After the KMT's exile across the Strait, however, granting full civic rights to all descendants of ROC nationals, regardless of their place of birth or residency, became untenable.

Today, only those ROC nationals with "household registration" (*huji* 戶籍) have the right to vote and to live in the territories governed by the ROC, also known as the "free area of the ROC," meaning Taiwan, Penghu, Matsu, Kinmen, Green Island, and Orchid Island.[20] Eligibility for household registration now typically requires proof that one's father or mother has held the same.[21] Still, the number of people eligible to apply for ROC nationality "without household registration," under the terms of the Nationality Act, is theoretically larger than even the population of Taiwan today, including those whose families did not settle in Taiwan in 1949 but escaped to Hong Kong, Macau, the Philippines, Thailand, Myanmar (formerly Burma), Vietnam, Indonesia, and South Korea; and those whose families left Taiwan from the 1950s onwards. Every discussion about alleviating demographic decline by lifting entry and residency restrictions for "ROC nationals without household registration" thus raises the specter of uncontrolled ethnic Chinese immigration, a repeat of the historical trauma by which more than one million people with no prior connection to Taiwan arrived in span of just a few years from the late 1940s to the early 1950s.

At mid-century, Taiwan was forced to accommodate a cross-Strait and globalized definition of Chinese identity. The resentment over this unchosen role makes the position of prospective new immigrants of "Chinese" or "Han" ethnicity a fraught one. In the spring of 2022, DPP lawmakers considered proposals by the Mainland Affairs Council to streamline the process for higher-earning professionals from Hong Kong to obtain permanent residency. These proposals were opposed by Taiwanese who fretted that it would be impossible to separate legitimate migrants from PRC spies. Despite broad support among Taiwanese for the protests in Hong Kong in 2019, worries that Hong Kongers themselves are still too "Chinese" in their identity or outlook, especially toward Taiwan, have stymied efforts to welcome more émigrés from the port city.[22] Skeptics also questioned why wealthier ethnic Chinese migrants should receive preferential treatment over migrants of different racial and ethnic backgrounds who have lived in Taiwan for far longer.

Yet there is limited public enthusiasm for large-scale reform that would allow migrants of all nationalities and socioeconomic levels a route to dual nationality and political participation. Although Taiwan is a settler colony, the ROC lacks the birthright citizenship laws of New World settler states like the United States and Canada. Children born in Taiwan to two foreign nationals have no automatic rights to residency, education, health care, or voting. Revisions to the Nationality Law in 2016 have made it possible for "high-level professionals" and individuals who made notable contributions to the country to receive ROC nationality and household registration without needing to renounce their first citizenship.[23] Yet the number of new dual citizens created as a result is so far miniscule: a total of only 198 in the first category as of August 2021.[24] Moreover, the income and career requirements ensure that most of these exceptional individuals are already over reproductive age (or in the case of clergy recognized for their service, committed to celibacy). Nor does their new legal status extend to their spouses or existing children. The 2016 amendments have therefore produced a handful of new Taiwanese people, but in all likelihood, no new Taiwanese families.

Taiwanese are proof that people of Han Chinese heritage do not need to support the establishment of a cross-Strait "one China." Yet even as some Taiwanese fret that ethnicity-based definitions of nationality and civic rights render them vulnerable to PRC infiltration and claims of ownership, Taiwanese society continues to be organized in ways that disadvantage and marginalize people of non-"Chinese" heritage. Since the early 1990s, Taiwan has become what Isabelle Cheng calls a "'migration state' with an open economy but a closed national community," an "expediency [that] enjoys consistent public endorsement."[25] According to the Ministry of Labor, as of October 2021, there were 680,571 "migrant workers" in Taiwan, the vast majority from Vietnam, Thailand, Indonesia, and the Philippines, laboring in "3D industries" (dangerous, difficult, and dirty), such as manufacturing, construction, agriculture, fishing, and domestic care for the young and elderly. Huynh Tam Sang, a Vietnamese scholar working on Southeast Asia-Taiwan relations, notes that "While these workers are helping [to] sustain the growth of Taiwan's economy, their rights and dignity often take second place after company profits... [The] infrastructure for addressing their concerns remains limited and often difficult to access."[26]

Migrant workers constitute a second-class population living in parallel to mainstream society, spending their (re)productive years in Taiwan but long denied viable, equitable pathways to permanent settlement and family establishment and reunion. Until 2022, the maximum amount of time a migrant worker could stay in Taiwan was fourteen years for those acting as domestic aides, and twelve for those working in other fields. In February 2022, the Executive Cabinet approved a plan that would allow migrant workers meeting stringent employment and salary requirements to be re-classified as "intermediate skilled manpower" after six years and be eligible for permanent residency in five more years. Unlike foreign white-collar professionals, migrant workers must often pay fees to brokers to secure initial employment, and they are not permitted to bring spouses or children to Taiwan with them. Domestic helpers, who are not covered by the Labor Standards Act, commonly live with their Taiwanese employers, a setup that results in pressure to overwork or complete tasks outside those contractually agreed upon.[27] Meanwhile, factory, construction, and fishery workers often live in crowded dormitories with few amenities and little privacy, where employers sometimes impose arbitrary rules on movement or behavior that do not apply to Taiwanese employees. In just one recent example, Amnesty International issued a report criticizing a June 2021 order by Miaoli County confining migrant workers to their dormitories during an outbreak of COVID-19.[28] The order was rescinded three weeks later after negative coverage in the local and international press.

The long-standing plight of migrant workers—which has been extensively documented yet arouses little domestic indignation—points to wariness among Taiwanese toward creating new citizens from a pool of people without historical ties to the island. Among Taiwanese, there is a sense that as their own identities are only newly consolidated and still under threat, welcoming cultural and ethnic "outsiders" on equal terms would upset hard-won social cohesion and the balance of power between the two major political parties in unpredictable ways. In addition, depressed salaries among Taiwanese also limit the empathy that locals have for foreign blue-collar workers, who are seen as benefiting from opportunities missing in their home countries.

In some respects, this state of affairs has persisted because Taiwan is now a democracy, where politicians and officials listen to *voters*, including brokers and employers, but not a rotating group of foreign laborers. Some migrant workers do marry Taiwanese spouses, acquire long-term residency, and raise Taiwanese families, adding to the population of overwhelmingly female Southeast Asian "new immigrants" who moved to Taiwan specifically for marriage. Since the 1990s, approximately ten to fourteen percent of children born in Taiwan have at least one foreign-born parent, a large percentage of whom are from Southeast Asia; in the future, they may be more primed to speak up about the concerns of "mixed" families and recent settlers from lower class or non-Sinophone backgrounds.[29]

The slow progress on integrating hundreds of thousands of young, working-age Southeast Asian workers points to a future in which fewer people qualify as sufficiently Taiwanese according to varying standards of lineage, "blood," family history, upbringing, politics, ideology, or self-identification, while Taiwan itself remains isolated and embattled. Simultaneously, the frequently poor and discriminatory treatment meted out to migrant workers undermines Taiwanese narratives about being a bulwark of democratic values and human rights in twenty-first century Asia. Comparing the trajectories of movements of immigrant labor rights in Taiwan, Korea, and Japan, Erin Aeran Chung argues that "instead of providing a receptive environment for immigrant incorporation, Taiwan's multiethnic society, long immigration history, cross-Strait politics, and contentious democratization process left migrants with few allies among state *and* civil-society actors who saw no place for them in Taiwan's democratic project."[30]

This represents the culmination of both decades of KMT legal and educational policies designed to mold the people of Taiwan into model Chinese and the trend toward "localization" (*bentuhua* 本土化) that has flourished post-democracy. In an essay diagnosing the long-term structural issues challenging Taiwan, political scientist Syaru Shirley Lin observes that the absolute dominance of Mandarin, combined with "the desire of many Taiwanese to consolidate a local identity, distinct from that in China," to ground themselves in once-stigmatized languages, practices, histories, and narratives associated with Taiwan itself, can leave little room for internationalization. "If Taiwan remains a parochial society," Lin warns, "it will find it has no natural connections to the world except through China."[31]

Whether Taiwanese will come to feel secure and confident enough in their identities to welcome in, socialize, and assimilate a new generation of much-needed immigrants and "new Taiwanese"—even if the ROC remains in place for geopolitical reasons—will be the real test of Taiwan's future survival and growth. If Taiwan does not want to be seen simply as a "Chinese democracy"—a distortion of how and why it democratized—giving a permanent stake in society to those who migrated from other parts of the world will be an important step toward breaking the linkage between ethnicity, heritage, and nationality that both the KMT and CCP have sought to impose on it. Taiwanese were not given a choice to accept the ROC, its Nationality Act, or its brand of Chinese ethnonationalism, nor to avoid being the target of the PRC's twenty-first century imperial ambitions. But the choice to cultivate a more diverse and eclectic national community today—one that will extend Taiwan's connections to communities and countries around the globe—lies with the people of Taiwan.

NOTES

1. Hsu, Chien, and Myers, "Can Taiwan Continue to fight off Chinese Disinformation?" For academic and think tank studies of Chinese disinformation and misinformation campaigns in Taiwan, see Hung and Hung, "How China's Cognitive Warfare Works"; and Dickey, "Confronting the Challenge of Online Disinformation in Taiwan.".
2. Wu, "Spectralizing the White Terror," 76.
3. Li and Song, "Taiwan as ghost island?" 285.
4. PTT was started by Taiwanese but in recent years has been infiltrated by Chinese bots and trolls.
5. Chang, Haider, and Ferrara, "Digital Civic Participation and Misinformation during the 2020 Taiwanese Presidential Election," 146.
6. Cheng, "Taiwan's Unexpectedly Crazy Dating App Scene."
7. Hioe, "The Dried Mango Strips of National Doom."
8. Ho, "'Dried Mango,'" 199.
9. Dirlik, "Taiwan," 2.
10. Election Study Center at National Chengchi University. *Taiwan/Chinese Identity 1992/06-2022/06.*.
11. Central Intelligence Agency, *The World Factbook*, "Field Listing – Birth rate."
12. Chou, "Taiwan's falling birthrate 'threatens its economic security.'".
13. Kao and Liu, "Taiwan to have world's lowest birthrate by 2035," 1.
14. Chou, "Taiwan's falling birthrate.".
15. Yang, The *Great Exodus*, 263.
16. Tsai, *Lee Teng-hui and Taiwan's Quest for Identity*, xii–xiii.
17. For more on the articulation of a multicultural "new Taiwanese" identity starting in the 1990s, see Timothy Ka-ying Wong, "From Ethnic to Civic Nationalism"; Damm, "The Multiculturalization of Taiwan"; and Brown, *Is Taiwan Chinese?* (in particular chapter 1, "What's in a Name? Culture, Identity, and the 'Taiwan Problem.'")
18. For more on "marriage migrants," see Tsay, "Marriage Migrants of Women from China and Southeast Asia to Taiwan."
19. Ministry of Justice, "Nationality Act."
20. Central Election Commission, *Characteristics of Taiwan Elections*.
21. Ministry of Justice, "Household Registration Act."

22. Kuo and Chen, "Taiwan offered hope after they fled Hong Kong. Now, they're leaving again."
23. Ministry of Justice, "Nationality Act."
24. Chien, "17 Senior High Professionals Naturalize as Taiwanese."
25. Cheng, "We want productive workers, not fertile women," 453.
26. Sang, "Addressing Challenges Faced by Taiwan's Migrant Workers."
27. Hsiao, "Groups urge law to protect migrant domestic workers."
28. Pan, "Miaoli migrant worker lockdown 'discriminatory.'"
29. Montlake, "The New Taiwanese."
30. Chung, *Immigrant Incorporation in East Asian Democracies*, 81.
31. Lin, "It's not just China."

Bibliography

Primary Sources

Government Documents, Data, and Communications

"Additional Articles of the Constitution of the ROC." Amended June 10, 2005. Laws and Regulations Database of the ROC (Taiwan), Ministry of Justice. https://law.moj.gov.tw/ENG/LawClass/LawAll.aspx?pcode=A0000002.

"Amendments to the Constitution of the Republic of China." Promulgated May 1, 1991. Law Bank. https://www.lawbank.com.tw/treatise/lawrela.aspx?lsid=FL000002&ldate=19910501&lno=1,2,6.

"Articles of the Broadcast and Television Act no longer in effect." Law Bank [Fayuan falü wang 法源法律網]. https://www.lawbank.com.tw/treatise/lawrela.aspx?lsid=FL016419&ldate=19820607&lno=19,20

Australian Government Department of Foreign Affairs and Trade. "U.S.-Australia-Japan Trilateral Strategic Dialogue." August 5, 2022. https://www.foreignminister.gov.au/minister/penny-wong/statements/us-australia-japan-trilateral-strategic-dialogue.

Bureau of Consular Affairs, ROC (Taiwan). "MOFA [Ministry of Foreign Affairs to release new passport to highlight TAIWAN in January 2021." September 4, 2020. https://www.boca.gov.tw/cp-220-5862-75d57-2.html.

"The Cairo Declaration." November 26, 1943. History and Public Policy Program Digital Archive. *Foreign Relations of the United States, Diplomatic Papers, the Conferences at Cairo and Tehran, 1943.* Washington, DC: United States Government Printing Office, 1961. 448–449. https://digitalarchive.wilsoncenter.org/document/122101.pdf?v=d41d8cd98f00b204e9800998ecf8427e.

Central Election Commission. *Characteristics of Taiwan Elections.* Amended November 3, 2017. https://web.cec.gov.tw/english/cms/ctw.

———. "2020 Presidential and Vice-Presidential Election." January 21, 2020. https://www.cec.gov.tw/english/cms/pe/32471.

———. "Zhongxuanhui fabu quanguo xing gongmin toupiao an di 7 an zhi di 16 an gongtou piao gao" 中選會發布全國性公民投票案第7案至第16案公投票告 [Announcement of the nationwide referendum measures 7 to 16 voting notice]. October 24, 2018. https://www.cec.gov.tw/central/cms/107news/28788.

———. "Zhongxuanhui fabu quanguo xing gongmin toupiao di 7 an zhi di 16 an toupiao jieguo gonggao" 中選會發布全國性公民投票第7案至16案投票結果公告 [Announcement of the results of the nationwide referendum measures 7 to 16]. November 30, 2018. https://www.cec.gov.tw/central/cms/107news/29588.

Central Government of the People's Republic of China. "Taiwan wenti yu xin shidai Zhongguo tongyi shiye" 台湾问题与新时代中国统一事业 [The Taiwan question and the work of China's reunification in the new era]. August 10, 2022. http://www.gov.cn/zhengce/2022-08/10/content_5704839.htm.

Central Intelligence Agency, The World Factbook, "Field Listing – Birth rate." https://www.cia.gov/the-world-factbook/field/birth-rate/.

Council of Indigenous Peoples [Yuanzhuminzu weiyuanhui 原住民族委員會], ROC (Taiwan). "Introduction of Indigenous Peoples: Amis." https://www.cip.gov.tw/en/tribe/grid-list/50AABE9D1284F664D0636733C6861689/info.html.

"Constitution of the Republic of China, October 10, 1923." Reprinted as Appendix E in William L. Tung, The Political Institutions of Modern China. The Hague: Martinus Nijhoff, 1964: 332–343.

Indigenous Historical Justice and Transitional Justice Committee. "Indigenous Peoples of Taiwan to President Xi Jinping of China." Translated from the Mandarin by Chi-hao Yo 游知澔, January 8, 2019. https://chihaoyo.medium.com/indigenous-peoples-of-taiwan-to-president-xi-jinping-of-china-4469d1a3bde6.

Mainland Affairs Council, ROC (Taiwan). Public's View on Cross-Strait Relations, August 2018 and October 2018. https://www.mac.gov.tw/en/cp.aspx?n=AABFF8BF9C7B8DB4.

Ministry of Foreign Affairs of the People's Republic of China. "Statement by the Ministry of Foreign Affairs of the People's Republic of China." August 2, 2022. https://www.fmprc.gov.cn/eng/zxxx_662805/202208/t20220802_10732293.html.

Ministry of Justice. "Household Registration Act," Amended January 21, 2021, Laws and Regulations Database of the ROC (Taiwan). https://law.moj.gov.tw/ENG/LawClass/LawAll.aspx?pcode=D0030006.

"Nationality Act." Amended December 15, 2021. Laws and Regulations Database of the ROC (Taiwan). https://law.moj.gov.tw/ENG/LawClass/LawHistory.aspx?pcode=D0030001.

National Statistics Office, ROC (Taiwan) [Zongji zixun wang 總計資訊網]. 2020 Population and Housing Census [Xingzhengyuan zhuji zong chu 2020 nian renkou ji zhuzhai pucha chubu zongji jieguo tiyao fenxi 行政院主計總處2020年人口及住宅普查初步總計結果提要分析]. https://www.stat.gov.tw/public/Attachment/1112143117MKFOK1MR.pdf.

"Open Letter to Taiwan Compatriots (January 1, 1979)." Standing Committee of the National People's Congress of the People's Republic of China. *Chinese Law and Government* 35, no. 2 (2002): 21–24.

"The Provisional Constitution of the Republic of China," *American Journal of International Law* 6, no. 3. Supplement: Official Documents (July 1912): 149–154. https://doi.org/10.2307/2212590.

"Provisional Constitution of the Republic of China for the Period of Political Tutelage, June 1, 1931." Reprinted as Appendix F in William L. Tung, The Political Institutions of Modern China. The Hague: Martinus Nijhoff, 1964: 343–349.

United Nations. *Charter of the United Nations and Statute of the International Court of Justice.* New York: United Nations Publications, 2015.

United States Department of State. "Increasing People's Republic of China Military Pressure Against Taiwan Undermines Regional Peace and Stability." Press statement, October 3, 2021. https://www.state.

gov/increasing-peoples-republic-of-china-military-pressure-against-taiwan-undermines-regional-peace-and-stability/.

———. Bureau of East Asian and Pacific Affairs. US Relations with Taiwan Fact Sheet. Updated May 28, 2022. https://www.state.gov/u-s-relations-with-taiwan/.

"Yuanzhuminzu yu Taiwan zhengfu xin de huoban guanxi" 原住民族與台灣政府新的夥伴關係 [New partnership between the government of Taiwan and Aboriginal nations]. Signed September 10, 1999. Reprinted online in the concluding remarks of the virtual exhibit "Renshi buluo ditu: jia de duozhong quanshi 認識部落地圖：家的多重詮釋 [Map for getting to know the tribes: The multiple meanings of home], by the Yuanzhumin shuwei bowuguan 原住民數位博物館 [Digital Museum of Taiwan Indigenous People], sponsored by Guoli Taiwan shiqian wenhua bowuguan 國立台灣史前文化博物館 [National Museum of Prehistory]. https://www.dmtip.gov.tw/web/page/detail?l1=8&l2=98&l3=57.

University, Inter-governmental, and Non-Governmental Organization Reports and Datasets

Election Study Center at National Chengchi University. *Taiwan/Chinese Identity 1992/06-2022/06.* https://esc.nccu.edu.tw/PageDoc/Detail?fid=7800&id=6961.

Hong Kong Public Opinion Research Institute. *Opinion on Independence of Taiwan*, July 2, 2019. https://www.pori.hk/pop-poll/taiwan-tibet-en/m003.html?lang=en.

International Olympics Committee. "Tokyo 2020 Medal Table." https://olympics.com/en/olympic-games/tokyo-2020/medals.

Johns Hopkins Coronavirus Research Center. *Taiwan Dataset.* https://coronavirus.jhu.edu/region/taiwan

Our World in Data. *Coronavirus (Covid-19) Vaccinations, Taiwan dataset.* https://ourworldindata.org/covid-vaccinations?country=TWN

World Health Organization. *Novel Coronavirus (2019-nCoV) Situation Report – 22,* February 11, 2020. https://www.who.int/docs/default-source/coronaviruse/situation-reports/20200211-sitrep-22-ncov.pdf.

Museums and Exhibitions

National Museum of Taiwan History (Guoli Taiwan Lishi Bowuguan 國立臺灣歷史博物館). "Architectural Features." https://www.nmth.gov.tw/en/archive?uid=298. Tainan.

———. Permanent Exhibition. Tainan.

———. "Skadang: [The] Place Where Molar Teeth Were Found," in "Place Names Tell Stories." Virtual exhibit. https://pnts.nmth.gov.tw/en/story/13. Tainan.

National Museum of Taiwan Literature (Guoli Taiwan Wenxue Guan 國立台灣文學館). *Bainian zhihou, cong yi kaishi* 百年之後，從一開始 [*The Abiding Light of a Century-old Beacon*]. Special Exhibition. Tainan.

Taiwan New Cultural Movement Memorial Museum [Taiwan xin wenhua yundong jinian guan 台灣新文化運動紀念館]. Permanent Exhibition. Taipei.

Zhongshan Hall (Zhongshan tang 中山堂). *Kang Ri zhanzheng shengli ji Taiwan guangfu jinian pai* 抗日戰爭勝利暨台灣光復紀念牌 [*Victory in the War Against Japan and the Retrocession of Taiwan*]. Permanent Monument. Taipei.

Announcements, Information, and Advertisements

Chiang Wei-shui's Cultural Foundation [Caituan faren Jiang Wei-shui wenhua jijinhui 財團法人蔣渭水文化基金會]. " Naxie tien, Jiang Wei-shui zai lao li" 那些天，蔣渭水在牢裡 [Cantata: Jail as my hotel]. http://www.weishui.org/p/1122-1930.html.

Kuomintang. "Russian Olympic Committee Flag Appearing Next to President Tsai's #ROC Tweet, Tsai Administration Should Convey its Concern." Press release. August 3, 2021. http://www.kmt.org.tw/2021/08/roc.html.

Ministry of the Interior [Neizheng bu 內政部], Construction and Planning Agency [Yingjian shu 營建署], ROC (Taiwan). "'Mountain Moon Bridge' Overcomes the Dangerous Obstacles of the Canyon and Wins the Public Construction Golden Quality Award." April 17, 2020. https://www.cpami.gov.tw/news/realtime-news/34889-Mountain-Moon-Bridge-Overcomes-the-Dangerous-Obstacles-of-the-Canyon-and-Wins-the-Public-Construction-Golden-Quality-Award.html.

National Taiwan Museum of Literature. "Wenxie bainian taiwen guan: 'bainian qingshu tezhan' yong qingshu chuandi wu qing shidao zhong de zhire xinyi" 文協百年 台文館「百年情書特展」用情書傳遞無情世道中的炙熱心意 [Centennial of the Cultural Association, National Taiwan Literature Museum's '100 years of love letters special exhibition', using love letters handed down to convey passion in a ruthless world]. https://www.nmtl.gov.tw/information?uid=194&pid=140203.

Qingtian 76. "Family and Personal Life: Professor Ting Yin H. Ma Family." December 21, 2022. https://www.qingtian76.tw/professor-t-y-ma-took-up-residence-in-professor-adachis-house/?lang=en.

TWBF Secretariat. "Statement on Taiwan Wild Bird Federation Name Change and Clarifications on Removal from BirdLife International." September 24, 2020. https://www.bird.org.tw/news/602

Multimedia and Social Media

Seven Network Broadcast of Tokyo 2020 Opening Ceremony, July 23, 2021, video clip, posted on Twitter by Mark Harrison. July 23, 2021, 10:49 p.m. https://twitter.com/mhar4/status/1418780451850776579

Cheng, Li-chun, and Wu Rwei-wen. "Ziyou yu zhengzhi – chengwei yige ziyou ren, xiangxiang women de gongtongti" 自由與政治 – 成為一個自由人，想像我們的共同體 [Liberty and government – To become a free person, imagining our community], October 13, 2021, in *Zheng Li-jun de sixiang caochang: ziyou liu jiang* 鄭麗君的思想操場：自由六講) [Cheng Li-chun's playground thoughts: Six episodes of free speaking]. Produced by Jing hao ting 鏡好聽 [Mirror Voice]. Podcast, 02:42. https://www.mirrorvoice.com.tw/podcasts/130/2196.

Chiang Wei-shui, "Taiwan wenhua xiehui hui ge" 台灣文化協會會歌 [Taiwan Cultural Association song]. Lyrics reprinted by the National Museum of Taiwan History. https://audio.nmth.gov.tw/audio/zh-TW/Item/Detail/ecac4148-9e1d-43a7-b2fe-70df8e45d07e.

Hong Kong Free Press. Twitter thread (40 Tweets, 34th Tweet), December 8, 2021, 2:49 a.m. https://twitter.com/hkfp/status/1203597518996566016.

Lin Ching-Yi. Twitter post, August 12, 2021, 1:55 a.m. https://twitter.com/minorta/status/1425712533722210304.

Lee, Yang. Facebook post, July 31, 2021, 9:24 a.m. https://www.facebook.com/leeyang0812/posts/pfbid02aEZawQakhJG1Sjm8bgZ4QYAminuP1pyAwf4a89fFePcaxqZcMTLEWSAZaaRfh5ful.

Lin, Fei-fan. "On 228, I choose to stand with Taiwan's Indigenous Peoples." Translated from the Mandarin and reprinted in *New Bloom Magazine*, March 6, 2017. https://newbloommag.net/2017/03/06/lin-fei-fan-228-indigenous/.

National Press Club of Australia, "HE Xiao Qian, Ambassador of the People's Republic of China, Address to the NPC," YouTube Video, August 12, 2022. https://www.youtube.com/watch?v=rsJ6RSyBHRQ.

Tsai, Ing-wen Spokesperson's Office [Xiao ying fayanren 小英發言人], "2020 "Wo hui huiqu toupiao, na ni ne?" Taiwan ban 2020 我會回去投票，那你呢? 台灣篇 [2020, I will go home to vote, what about you? Taiwan edition]. December 24, 2019, YouTube Video, 0:09 and 1:07, https://www.youtube.com/watch?v=CpNG-dHrNKQ.

Wang, Xiaojian. Twitter thread (6 Tweets). October 10, 2021, 6:46 a.m. https://twitter.com/ChinaSpox_India/status/1447166662222901258.

Live Speeches

Chen, Shui-bian. "2006 nian 'guo zhong you guo: xianfa yuanzhuminzu zhuan zhang' xueshu yanjiu tao hui" kaimu dianli zhici" 「2006 年『國中有國：憲法原住民族專章』學術研究討會」開幕典禮致詞 [A state within a state: The chapter of the Aborigines in Taiwan's [*sic*] constitution]. Speech, November 18, 2006. Reprinted in *Chen Shui-bian zongtong xiansheng jiushiwu nian yanlun*

xuanji (*shang*) 陳水扁總統先生九十五年言論選集 (上) [The col-
lection of President Chen Shui-bien's speech, vol. 1], 104–106. Taipei:
The Government Information Office, Executive Yuan, 2007..

Harper, Stephen. "Statement of apology to former students of Indian
Residential Schools." Speech, Ottawa, June 11, 2008. Government
of Canada. https://www.rcaanc-cirnac.gc.ca/eng/1100100015644/157
1589171655.

Rudd, Kevin. "2008: National Apology to the Stolen Generations." Speech,
Canberra, February 13, 2008. Parliament of Australia. https://www.aph.
gov.au/Visit_Parliament/Art/Exhibitions/Custom_Media/Apology_
to_Australias_Indigenous_Peoples.

Tsai, Ing-wen. "Full text of Taiwan President Tsai Ing-wen's acceptance
speech." Speech, Taipei, January 11, 2020. Office of the President,
ROC (Taiwan). https://focustaiwan.tw/politics/202001110014.

———. "President Tsai Apologizes Indigenous Peoples on Behalf of
Government." Speech, Taipei, August 1, 2016. Office of the President,
ROC (Taiwan). https://english.president.gov.tw/NEWS/4950.

———. "President Tsai delivers 2021 National Day Address." Speech,
Taipei, October 10, 2020. Office of the President, ROC (Taiwan).
https://english.president.gov.tw/News/6175.

Xi, Jinping, "Working Together to Realize Rejuvenation of the Chinese
Nation and Advance China's Peaceful Reunification." Speech, Beijing,
January 2, 2019. Taiwan Work Office of the CPC Central Committee,
Taiwan Affairs Office of the State Council. http://www.gwytb.gov.
cn/wyly/201904/t20190412_12155687.htm.

Memoirs

Davidson, James W. *The Island of Formosa, Past and Present: History, People, Resources, and Commercial Prospects.* New York: Macmillan & Co.,
1903.

Kerr, George. *Formosa Betrayed.* Manchester, UK: Camphor Press, 2018.

Lee, Jessica J. *Two Trees Make a Forest: In Search of My Family's Past Among Taiwan's Mountains and Coasts.* New York: Catapult Books, 2020.

Peng, Min-min. *A Taste of Freedom.* Manchester, UK: Camphor Press, 2017.

SECONDARY SOURCES

Books

Monographs

Allen, Joseph. *Taipei: City of Displacements.* Seattle: University of Washington Press, 2012.

Alsford, Niki. *Transitions to Modernity in Taiwan: The Spirit of 1895 and the Cession of Formosa to Japan.* New York: Routledge, 2017.

Andrade, Tonio. *How Taiwan Became Chinese: Dutch, Spanish, and Han Colonization in the Seventeenth Century.* New York: Columbia University Press, 2008.

Barclay, Paul. *Outcasts of Empire: Japan's Rule on Taiwan's "Savage Border," 1874–1945.* Oakland, CA: University of California Press, 2018.

Berry, Michael. *The Musha Incident.* New York: Columbia University Press, 2022.

Blundell, David. *Austronesian Taiwan: Linguistics, History, Ethnology, Prehistory.* Taipei, Taiwan: Sheng Ye Museum of Formosan Aborigines, 2009.

Brown, Melissa. *Is Taiwan Chinese?: The Impact of Culture, Power, and Migration on Changing Identities.* Los Angeles: University of California Press, 2004.

Carrai, Maria Adele. *Sovereignty in China: A Genealogy of a Concept Since 1840.* Cambridge: Cambridge University Press, 2019.

Chen, Tsui-lien, *Zizhi zhi meng: Rizhi shiqi dao ererba de Taiwan minzhu yundong* 自治之夢：日治時期到二二八的台灣民主運動

[The dream of self-governance: Taiwanese democracy movements from Japanese colonialism to February 28th]. Taipei: Spring Hill Publishers [Chun shan chuban youxian gongsi 春山出版有限公司], 2020.

Ching, Leo T. S. *Anti-Japan: The Politics of Sentiment in Postcolonial East Asia*. Durham, NC: Duke University Press, 2021.

Chiu, Hsin-hui. *The Colonial 'Civilizing Process' in Dutch Formosa, 1624–1662*. Leiden: Brill, 2008.

Chung, Erin Aeran. *Immigrant Incorporation in East Asian Democracies*. Cambridge: Cambridge University Press, 2020.

Dawley, Evan. *Becoming Taiwanese: Ethnogenesis in a Colonial City, 1880s–1950s*. Cambridge, MA: Harvard University Asia Center, 2019.

Denton, Kirk. *The Landscape of Historical Memory: The Politics of Museums and Memorial Culture in Post-Martial Law Taiwan*. Hong Kong: Hong Kong University Press, 2021.

Harrison, Mark. *Legitimacy, Meaning, and Knowledge in the Making of Taiwanese Identity*. New York: Palgrave Macmillan, 2006.

Horne, John, and Garry Whannel. *Understanding the Olympics*. Milton Park, UK: Taylor and Francis, 2016.

Hsiau, A-chin. *Contemporary Taiwanese Cultural Nationalism*. London, UK: Routledge, 2005.

———. *Politics and Cultural Nativism in 1970s Taiwan: Youth, Narrative, Nationalism*. New York: Columbia University Press, 2021.

Hung, Li-wan 洪麗完. *Shufan shehui wangle yu jiti yishi: Taiwan zhongbu pingpuzuqun lishi bianqian, 1700–1900* 熟番社會網路與集體意識：台灣中部平埔族群歷史變遷, 1700–1900 [The relationship of social networks and ethnic identities for Shufan: The historical transformation of Plains Aborigines in central Taiwan under Qing rule, 1700–1900]. New Taipei City: Lian jing chu ban 聯經出版 [Linking Publishing Company], 2009.

Hutchings, Kimberly. *Time and World Politics: Thinking the Present*. Manchester, UK: Manchester University Press, 2008.

Jacobs, J. Bruce. *Democratizing Taiwan*. Leiden: Brill, 2012.

———. *The Kaohsiung Incident in Taiwan and Memoirs of a Foreign Big Beard*. Leiden: Brill, 2016.

Kerr, George. *Formosa: Licensed Revolution and the Home Rule Movement, 1895–1945*. Honolulu, HI: University of Hawaii Press, 1974.

Lim, Louisa. *Indelible City: Dispossession and Defiance in Hong Kong*. New York: Riverhead Books, 2022.

Lin, Hsiao-ting. *Accidental State: Chiang Kai-shek, the United States, and the Making of Taiwan*. Cambridge, MA: Harvard University Press, 2016.

Lin, Sylvia Li-chun. *Representing Atrocity in Taiwan: the 2/28 Incident and White Terror in Fiction and Film*. New York: Columbia University Press, 2007.

Metzler, John J. *Taiwan's Transformation: 1895 to the Present*. New York: Palgrave Macmillan, 2017.

Munsterhjelm, Mark. *Living Dead in the Pacific: Contested Sovereignty and Racism in Genetic Research on Taiwan Aborigines*. Chicago: University of Chicago Press, 2014.

Phillips, Steven E. *Between Assimilation and Independence: The Taiwanese Encounter Nationalist China, 1945–1950*. Stanford, CA: Stanford University Press, 2003.

Rigger, Shelley. *From Opposition to Power: Taiwan's Democratic Progressive Party*. Boulder, CO: Lynne Rienner Publishers, 2001.

Shepherd, John. *Statecraft and Political Economy on the Taiwan Frontier, 1600–1800*. Stanford, CA: Stanford University Press, 1993.

Simon, Scott. *Truly Human: Indigeneity and Indigenous Resurgence on Formosa*. Toronto: University of Toronto Press, 2023.

Sullivan, Jonathan, and Lev Nachman. *Taiwan: A Contested Democracy Under Threat*. Newcastle upon Tyne, UK: Agenda Publishing, 2023).

Teng, Emma. *Taiwan's Imagined Geography: Chinese Colonial Travel Writing and Pictures, 1683–1895*. Cambridge, MA: Harvard University Asia Center, 2004.

Tsai, Shih-shan Henry. *Lee Teng-hui and Taiwan's Quest for Identity*. New York: Palgrave Macmillan, 2005.

Tsurumi, E. Patricia. *Japanese Colonial Education in Taiwan, 1895–1945*. Cambridge, MA: Harvard University Press, 1977.

Wasserstrom, Jeff. *Vigil: Hong Kong on the Brink*. New York: Columbia Global Reports, 2020.

Xu, Guoqi. *Olympic Dreams: China and Sports, 1895–2008*. Cambridge, MA: Harvard University Press,

2008.

Yang, Dominic Meng-Hsuan. *The Great Exodus: Trauma, Memory, and Identity in Modern Taiwan*. Cambridge: Cambridge University Press, 2021.

Edited Collections

Non-fiction

Beckershoff, André. "The Sunflower Movement: Origins, structures, and strategies of Taiwan's resistance against the 'Black Box.'" In *Taiwan's Social Movements under Ma Ying-jeou*, edited by Dafydd Fell, 113–134. London: Routledge, 2017.

Chan, Holmes, ed. *Aftershock: Essays from Hong Kong*. Hong Kong: Small Tune Press, 2020.

Chen, Chia-li Chen. "Museums and National History in Conflict: Two Case Studies in Taiwan." In *A Companion to Public History*, edited by David Dean, 441–454. Hoboken, NJ: Wiley Blackwell, 2018.

Chen, Edward, I-te. "The attempt to integrate the empire: legal perspectives." In *The Japanese Colonial Empire, 1895–1945*, edited by Ramon H. Myers and Mark R. Peattie, 240–274. Princeton: Princeton University Press, 1984.

Chen, Yi-shen. "From a Province to a Sovereign State: Taiwan's Political Changes as Reflected in the Three Critical Years 1951, 1971, and 1991." In *A Century of Development in Taiwan: From Colony to Modern*

State, edited by Peter C. Y. Chow, 40–59. Cheltenham: Edward Elgar, 2022.

Chiu, Kui-fen, Dafydd Fell, and Lin Ping, eds. *Migration to and From Taiwan*. London: Routledge, 2014.

Damm, Jens. "The Multiculturalization of Taiwan: From a Unified Han-Identity to the 'Four Great Ethnic Groups.'" In *The Globalization of Confucius and Confucianism*, edited by Klaus Mühlhahn and Nathalie van Looy, 72–89. Berlin: Lit Verlag, 2012.

Hsieh, Jolan (Bavaragh Dagalomi). "Restoring Pingpu Indigenous Status and Rights," *Taiwan's Contemporary Indigenous Peoples*, edited by Chia-yuan Huang, Daniel Davies, and Dafydd Fell, 239–255. New York: Routledge, 2021.

Kollar, Justin. "Cultivating (post)colonialism: Architecture, Landscape, and the politics of the Taiwan Sugar Corporation." In *Neocolonialism and Built Heritage: Echoes of Empire in Africa, Asia, and Europe*, edited by Daniel E. Coslett, 236–256. New York: Routledge, 2019.

Liao, Ping-hui. "Print Culture and the Emergent Public Sphere in Colonial Taiwan, 1895–1945." In *Taiwan Under Japanese Colonial Rule, 1895-1945: History, Culture, Memory*, edited by Liao Ping-hui and David Der-wei Wang, 78–94. New York: Columbia University Press, 2006.

Morris, Andrew D., ed., *Japanese Taiwan: Colonial Rule and its Contested Legacy*. London: Bloomsbury Academic, 2015.

Ngo, T.W., and Hong-zen Wang, eds. *Politics of Difference in Taiwan*. New York, Routledge, 2011.

Simon, Scott. "Making Natives: Japan and the Creation of Indigenous Formosa." In *Japanese Taiwan: Colonial Rule and its Contested Legacy*, edited by Andrew D. Morris, 75–92. London: Bloomsbury Academic, 2015.

Tsai, Chia-hung. "Who is the Taiwan Voter?" In *The Taiwan Voter*, edited by Christopher H. Achen and T.Y. Wang, 26–44. Ann Arbor, Michigan: University of Michigan Press, 2017. https://library.oapen.org/bitstream/handle/20.500.12657/24046/1006087.pdf.

Tsay, Ching-lung. "Marriage Migrants of Women from China and Southeast Asia to Taiwan." In *(Un)tying the Knot: Ideal and Reality in Asian Marriage*, edited by Gavin W. Jones and Kamalini Ramdas, 173–191. Singapore: Asia Research Institute, National University of Singapore, 2004.

Uradyn Bulag. "Nationality 民族." In *Afterlives of Chinese Communism*, edited by Christian Sorace, Ivan Franceschini, and Nicholas Loubere, 149–154. Canberra: ANU Press, 2020.

Fiction

Goldblatt, Howard, and Sylvia Li-chun Lin, eds., *A Son of Taiwan: Stories of Government Atrocity*. Amherst: NY: Cambria Press, 2021.

Rowen, Ian, ed., *Transitions in Taiwan: Stories of the White Terror*. Amherst, NY: Cambria Press, 2021.

Book Excerpts

Chen, Tsui-lien 陳翠蓮. "Taiwan shi Taiwanren de Taiwan: wenming, ziyou, zunyan: 1920 niandai Taiwanren de zizhi zhi meng" 台灣是台灣人的台灣：文明、自由、尊嚴，1920年代台灣人的自治之夢 [Taiwan belongs to the Taiwanese: Civilization, liberty, dignity, the Taiwanese dream of self-governance in the 1920s], The Reporter 報導者, August 8, 2020. https://www.twreporter.org/a/bookreview-taiwan-democratization-movement-under-japanese-rule.

Ho, Ming-sho. "The Activist Legacy of Taiwan's Sunflower Movement," *Carnegie Endowment for International Peace*, August 8, 2018. https://carnegieendowment.org/2018/08/02/activist-legacy-of-taiwan-s-sunflower-movement-pub-76966.

Peer-Reviewed Academic Articles

Barclay, Paul D. "Peddling Postcards and Selling Empire: Image-Making in Taiwan under Japanese Colonial Rule." *Japanese Studies* 30, no. 1 (May 2010): 81–110. https://doi.org/10.1080/10371391003639138

Brady, Anne-Marie. "Unifying the Ancestral Land: The CCP's 'Taiwan' Frames." *The China Quarterly* 223 (September 2015): 787–806. https://doi.org/10.1017/S030574101500082X.

Chan, Gerald. "The 'Two Chinas' Problem and the Olympic Formula." *Pacific Affairs* 48, no. 3 (Autumn 1985): 473–490.

Chang, Bi-yu. "So close, yet so far away: Imaging Chinese 'homeland' in Taiwan's geography education (1945–68)." *Cultural Geographies* 18, no. 3 (2010): 385–411.

Chang, Ho-chun Herbert, Samar Haider, and Emilio Ferrara, "Digital Civic Participation and Misinformation during the 2020 Taiwanese Presidential Election," *Media and Communication* 9, no. 1 (2021): 144-157.

Chen, Edward I-te. "Formosan Political Movements Under Japanese Colonial Rule, 1914–1937." *Journal of Asian Studies* 31, no. 3 (May 1972): 477–497.

Cheng, Isabelle. "We want productive workers, not fertile women: The expediency of employing Southeast Asian caregivers in Taiwan." *Asia Pacific Viewpoint* 61, no. 3 (2020): 453–465.

Clulow, Adam. "The Art of Claiming: Possession and Resistance in Early Modern Asia." *American Historical Review* 121, no. 1 (February 2016): 17–38. https://doi.org/10.1093/ahr/121.1.17.

Dirlik, Arif. "Taiwan: The Land Colonialisms Made." *boundary 2* 45, no. 3 (2018): 1–25. https://doi.org/10.1215/01903659-6915545.

Domes, Jürgen. "The 13th Party Congress of the Kuomintang: Towards Political Competition?" *The China Quarterly*, no. 118 (June 1989): 345–359. https://www.jstor.org/stable/pdf/654830.pdf.

Eckert, Amy E. "Constructing States: The Role of the International Community in the Creation of New States." *Journal of Public and International Affairs* 13 (Spring 2002): 19–39.

Edmonds, Richard Louis. "Aspects of the Taiwanese Landscape in the 20th Century." *The China Quarterly*, no. 165 (March 2001): 1–18. https://doi.org/10.1017/S0009443901000018.

Heé, Nadine. "Taiwan under Japanese Rule: Showpiece of a Model Colony? Historiographical Tendencies in Narrating Colonialism." *History Compass* 12, no. 8 (2014): 632–641.

Ho, Ming-sho. "'Dried Mango': Taiwan's Fiercely Democratic Young Voters." *Journal of the European Association for Chinese Studies* 2 (2021): 197–203. https://doi.org/10.25365/jeacs.2021.2.197-203.

Hung, Tzu-Chieh, and Tzu-Wei Hung. "How China's Cognitive Warfare Works: A Frontline Perspective of Taiwan's Anti-Disinformation Wars." *Journal of Global Security Studies* 7, no. 4 (2020): 1–18. https://doi-org.grinnell.idm.oclc.org/10.1093/jogss/ogac016.

Jacobs, J. Bruce. "Whither Taiwanization? The Colonization, Democratization, and Taiwanization of Taiwan." *Japanese Journal of Political Science* 14, no. 4 (December 2013): 567–586.

Jacobs, J. Bruce, and I-Hao Ben Liu, "Lee Teng-hui and the Idea of 'Taiwan.'" *The China Quarterly* 190 (June 2007): 375–393. https://doi.org/10.1017/S0305741007001245.

Kang, Peter. "From Cairo to the nationalistic geography of China: Street-naming in Taipei City immediately after WWII." *Onoma* 51: 45–74. https://doi.org/10.34158/ONOMA.51/2016/4.

Katz, Paul R. "Governmentality and its Consequences in Colonial Taiwan." *Journal of Asian Studies* 64, no. 2 (May 2005): 387–424. https://doi.org/10.1017/S0021911805000823.

Kuo, Cheng-tian. "Taiwan's Distorted Democracy in Comparative Perspective." *International Studies in* Sociology and Social Anthropology 77 (January 2000): 85–111. https://doi.org/10.1163/9789004473584_007.

Kuo, Su-Chiu. "From the Rover Incident to the Nanjia Treaty – Whose Conflict? Whose Treaty?" *Cultural and Religious Studies* 7, no. 12 (December 2019): 668–677. https://doi.org/10.17265/2328-2177/2019.12.003.

Kuo, Yawen, and Takafumi Shimizu. "Plan composition and actual conditions of official university residences in former Showa-Cho during the Japanese colonial period in Taiwan." *Japan Architectural*

Review 3, no. 2 (April 2020): 145–265. https://doi.org/10.1002/2475-8876.12141.

Li, Yao-tai, and Yunya Song. "Taiwan as ghost island? Ambivalent articulation of marginalized identities in computer-mediated discourses." *Discourse & Society* 3, no. 3 (2020): 285-306. https://doi.org/10.1177/0957926519889124.

Mao, Chin-ju. "Fashioning curriculum reform as identity politics – Taiwan's dilemma of curriculum reform in new millennium." *International Journal of Educational Development* 28, no. 5 (September 2008): 585–595.

Mona, Awi. "International Perspective on the Constitutionality of Indigenous People's Rights." *Taiwan International Studies Quarterly* (*Taiwan guoji yanjiu jikan* 台灣國際研究季刊) 3, no. 2 (Summer 2007): 85–139. http://www.tisanet.org/quarterly/3-2-4.pdf.

———. "Conceptualizing Indigenous Historical Justice Toward a Mutual Reconciliation with [the] State in Taiwan." *Washington International Law Journal* 28, no. 3 (2019): 653–675. https://digitalcommons.law.uw.edu/wilj/vol28/iss3/7.

Nachman, Lev. "Misalignment between Social Movements and Political Parties in Taiwan's 2016 Election: Not All Grass Roots are Green." *Asian Survey* 58, no. 5 (September/October 2018): 874–897.

Rowen, Ian. "Crafting the Taiwan Model for Covid-19: An Exceptional State in Pandemic Territory." *The Asia-Pacific Journal: Japan Focus* 28, issue 14, no. 9 (July 2020): 1–12. https://apjjf.org/-Ian-Rowen/5423/article.pdf.

———. "Inside Taiwan's Sunflower Movement: Twenty-four days in a student-occupied parliament, and the future of the region." *The Journal of Asian Studies* 74, no. 1 (February 2015): 5–21. https://doi.org/10.1017/S0021911814002174.

Sandel, Todd L. "Linguistic Capital in Taiwan: The KMT's Mandarin Language Policy and its perceived impact on language practices of bilingual Mandarin and Tai-gi Speakers." *Language in Society* 32, no. 4 (September 2003): 523–551.

Shih, Vincent Chang-an 施長安. "Dushi baocun: hou zhimin dushi zhengzhi xipu xue yi si si nan cun wei ge an yanjiu 都市保存：後殖民都市政治係譜學以四四南村為個案研究 [Urban conservation: Genealogy of postcolonial urban politics with "Shi-shi South Village Preservation Project" as case study]. *Chengshi yu sheji xue bao* 城市與設計學報 [Bulletin of cities and designs] 13 & 14 (March 2003): 395–409. https://doi.org/10.300008/CD.200303.0013.

Sia, Ek-hong Ljavakaw. "Crafting Aboriginal Nations in Taiwan: The Presbyterian Church and the Imagination of the Aboriginal National Subject." *Asian Studies Review* 42, no. 2 (2018): 356–375. https://doi.org/10.1080/10357823.2018.1444732.

Simon, Scott. "Negotiating Power: Elections and the Constitution of Indigenous Taiwanese." *American Ethnologist* 37, no. 4 (November 2010): 726–740. https://doi.org/10.1111/j.1548-1425.2010.01281.x.

Speidel, William M. "The Administrative and Fiscal Reforms of Liu Ming-ch'uan in Taiwan, 1884–1891: Foundation for Self-Strengthening." *Journal of Asian Studies* 35, no. 3 (May 1976): 441–459. https://doi.org/10.2307/2053275.

Sugimoto, Tomonori. "Urban Settler Colonialism: Policing and Displacing Indigeneity in Taipei, Taiwan." *City & Society* 31, no. 2 (August 2019): 227–250. https://doi.org/10.1111/ciso.12210.

Taylor, Jeremy E. "Colonial Takao: The Making of a Southern Metropolis." *Urban History*, 31, no. 1 (2004): 48–71.

Wang, Jason C., Chun Y. Ng, and Robert H. Brook. "Response to Covid-19 in Taiwan: Big Data Analytics, New Technology, and Proactive Testing." *Journal of the American Medical Association* 323, no. 14 (2020): 1341–1342. https://jamanetwork.com/journals/jama/article-abstract/2762689.

Wong, Timothy Ka-ying Wong. "From Ethnic to Civic Nationalism: The Formation and Changing Nature of Taiwanese Identity." *Asian Perspective* 25, no. 3 (2011): 175–206.

Wu, Chia-rong. "Spectralizing the White Terror: Horror, Trauma, and the Ghost-Island Narrative in *Detention*." *Journal of Chinese Cinemas* 15, no. 1 (2021): 73–86. https://doi.org/10.1080/17508061.2021.1926156.

Wu, Ming-hsuan. "Language Planning and Policy in Taiwan: Past, Present, and Future." *Language Problems and Language Planning* 35, no. 1 (January 2011): 15–34.

Wu, Ping-sheng. "Walking in Colonial Taiwan: A Study on Urban Modernization of Taipei, 1895-1945." *Journal of Asian Architecture and Building Engineering* 9, no. 2 (2010): 307–314. https://doi.org/1 0.3130/jaabe.9.307.

Wu, Ping-sheng, and Min-fu Hsu. "Phantasmagoric Venues from the West to the East: Studies on the Great Exhibition (1851) and the Taiwan Exhibition (1935)." *Journal of Asian Architecture and Building Engineering* 5, no. 2 (2006): 237–244. https://doi.org/10.3130/jaabe. 5.237.

Yang, Dominic Meng-Hsuan, and Mau-Kuei Chang. "Understanding the Nuances of Waishengren: History and Agency," in "Taiwan: the Consolidation of a Democratic and Distinct Society," edited by Paul Jobin and Frank Muyard, special issue, *China Perspectives* 83, no. 3 (September 2010): 108–122.

Encyclopedia Entries

Barclay, Paul D. "Japanese Empire in Taiwan." In The Oxford Research Encyclopedia on Asian History, ed. David Ludden. Oxford: Oxford University Press, 2020. https://doi.org/10.1093/acrefore/9780190277 727.013.376.

Lechner, Silviya. "Anarchy in International Relations." In The Oxford Research Encyclopedia on International Studies, ed. Nukhet Sandal. (Oxford, UK: Oxford University Press, 2022). https://doi.org/10.1093 /acrefore/9780190846626.013.79

Dissertations

Chang, Hui Ju. "Victorian Japan in Taiwan: Transmission and Impact of the 'Modern' upon the Architecture of Japanese Authority, 1853–1919." PhD thesis, University of Sheffield, 2014.

Hung, Chun-chi. "A Postcolonial Perspective on the State's Registration of Traditional Cultural Expressions." PhD thesis, Queen Mary University, London, 2019. https://qmro.qmul.ac.uk/xmlui/bitstream/handle/123456789/58585/Thesis_Chun%20Chi%20HUNG_final_signature%20omitted.pdf?sequence=8.

Kuo, Yen-kuang. "The History and Politics of Taiwan's February 28 Incident, 1947–2008." PhD thesis, University of Victoria, 2020. http://dspace.library.uvic.ca/bitstream/handle/1828/12556/Kuo_Yen-Kuang_PhD_2020.pdf.

Su, Huang-lan. "Writing 'Taiwanese': The pe̍h-ōe-jī Romanization and Identity Construction in Taiwan, 1860s–1990s." PhD thesis, University of Illinois at Urbana-Champaign, 2015. https://www.ideals.illinois.edu/items/89543.

Conference Presentations and Working Papers

Chen, Wei-lin, Ming-jen Lin, and Tzu-ting Yang. "Curriculum and National Identity: Evidence from the 1997 Curriculum Reform in Taiwan." Working Paper, November 4, 2018. https://econ.ntu.edu.tw/uploads/asset/data/5bff56c348b8a17fcd002283/hist_1071220.pdf.

Lien, Pei-te. "Comparing Sources and Patterns of Racial and Ethnic Formation in Taiwan and among Chinese/Taiwanese Americans." Conference paper. Annual Conference of the American Association for Chinese Studies, Baltimore, Maryland, October 5–7, 2018. http://taiwanfellowship.ncl.edu.tw/files/scholar_publish/1665-icpwkutyrmltskv.pdf.

Rigger, Shelley. "Democratic Transition and Consolidation in Taiwan." Conference paper. Taiwan's Future in the Asian Century: Towards a Strong, Prosperous, and Enduring Democracy Conference, American Enterprise Institute, Washington D.C., November 10, 2011. https://

www.aei.org/wp-content/uploads/2012/08/-democratic-transition-and-consolidation-in-taiwan_122745967872.pdf.

Simon, Scott. "Taiwan's Indigenized Constitution: What Place for Aboriginal Formosa?" Conference paper. Conference of the European Association of Taiwan Studies, Ruhr-Universitaet Bochum, April 1–2, 2005. https://www.tisanet.org/quarterly/2-1-12.pdf.

Newspaper and Magazine Articles

Blanchard, Ben. "Taiwan Accuses China of bullying over World Cup name change," *Reuters*, June 20, 2022.

Cady, Steve. "Canada Softens on Taiwan, Start of Olympics Assured." *New York Times*, July 15, 1976, A1.

Chambers, James. "Calm Before a Storm." *Monocle*, March 21, 2019. https://monocle.com/magazine/issues/122/calm-before-a-storm/.

Chan, Wilfred. "The WHO Ignores Taiwan. The World Pays the Price." *The* Nation, April 3, 2020. https://www.thenation.com/article/world/taiwan-who-coronavirus-china/.

Chen, Yu-fu, and Kayleigh Madjar. "Removal of Chiang statue prioritized." *Taipei Times*, September 9, 2021, p. 1. https://www.taipeitimes.com/News/front/archives/2021/09/09/2003764058.

Chen, Yu-fu, and Jake Chung, "Exhibition to show redesigns for Chiang Kai-shek Memorial Park." *Taipei Times,* April 29, 2022, p. 3. https://www.taipeitimes.com/News/taiwan/archives/2022/04/29/2003777422.

Cheng, Wei 鄭媁, Liu Wan-lin 劉宛琳, Chiu Tsai-wei 丘采薇, and Lee Cheng-ying 李承穎. "Guo qingzhu shijue wei jian guoqi, guohao bei yi 'yingwen taidu'" 國慶主視覺未見國旗、國號被疑「英文台獨」 [National flag and name are not seen in the visuals for National Day, suspected of [promoting] independence in English]. *Lianhe bao* 聯合報 [*United Daily News*], September 9, 2021. https://udn.com/news/story/6656/5732521.

Cheung, Han. "Taiwan in Time: The Struggle for a Proper Name." *Taipei Times*, July 30, 2017, p. 8. http://www.taipeitimes.com/News/feat/

archives/2017/07/30/2003675571#:~:text=On%20Aug.,to%20a%20long
%2Dmistreated%20people.

———. "Taiwan in Time: Fractured Resistance." *Taipei Times*, August
12, 2018, p. 8. https://www.taipeitimes.com/News/feat/archives/201
8/08/12/2003698377.

———. "Taiwan in Time: How many Zhongshan Halls were built in Taiwan?" *Taipei Times*, November 21, 2021, p. 13.

Chian hui-ru 簡惠茹. "17 gao zhuan rencai guihua Taiwan" 17 高專人
才歸化台灣 [17 senior high professionals naturalize as Taiwanese].
Ziyou shibao 自由時報 [*Liberty Times*], August 26, 2021. https://news.
ltn.com.tw/news/life/breakingnews/3651647.

"Chiang Wan-an wins Taipei for KMT in tight three-way mayoral
race." *Focus Taiwan (CNA English News)*, November 26, 2022. https://
focustaiwan.tw/politics/202211260026.

Chien, Amy Chang. "Taiwan's gold medal win over China in badminton
raises tensions." *New York Times*, August 1, 2021. https://www.
nytimes.com/2021/08/01/sports/olympics/badminton-gold-taiwan-
china.html.

Chou, Cybil. "Taiwan's falling birthrate 'threatens its economic security.'"
Nikkei Asia, July 18, 2021. https://asia.nikkei.com/Life-Arts/Life/
Taiwan-s-falling-birthrate-threatens-its-economic-security2.

"Commemoration the 110th anniversary of the 1911 Revolution was held
in Beijing, Xi Jinping delivered an important speech with Li Keqiang Li
Zhanshu Wang Huning Zhao Leji Han Zheng Wang Qishan attending,
chaired by Wang Yang." *Xinhua* News Agency, October 9, 2010. http://
www.news.cn/politics/2021-10/09/c_1127941553.htm.

"Crowdfunded 'Taiwan Can Help' ad published in New York Times."
Focus Taiwan (CNA English News), April 14, 2020. https://focustaiwan.
tw/society/202004140024.

"Daan senlin gongyuan yiqian zhang zhe yang! Taibei ren: zhule 30 nian
xianzai cai zhidao" 大安森林公園以前長這樣！台北人：住了30年
現在才知道 [Da'an Forest Park used to be this way! Taipei residents:
I lived here 30 years and only now knew]. *Lianhe xinwen wang* 聯合

新聞網 [*United Daily News Online*], December 12, 2019. https://news. housefun.com.tw/news/article/199010243517.html.

Durdin, Peggy. "Terror in Taiwan." *The Nation*. May 24, 1947, pp. 626–628.

Durdin, Tillman. "Formosa killings are put at 10,000." *New York Times*, March 29, 1947, p. 6.

Ellis, Samson. "China Claims Diplomatic Coup over Taiwan with Solomon Switch." *Bloomberg*, September 16, 2019. https://www.bloomberg.com/ news/articles/2019-09-16/solomon-islands-switches-ties-to-china-in-latest-blow-to-taiwan.

Gerber, Abraham. "Protesters decry Aboriginal land policy proposal." *Taipei Times*, February 24, 2017, p. 3. https://taipeitimes.com/News/ taiwan/archives/2017/02/24/2003665611.

Hale, Erin. "'Always campaign time': Why Taiwan's indigenous people back KMT." *Al Jazeera*, January 9, 2020. https://www. aljazeera.com/news/2020/1/9/always-campaign-time-why-taiwans-indigenous-people-back-kmt.

———. "Taiwan's Enduring Fascination with Japanese Architecture." *Nikkei Asia*, October 31, 2021. https://asia.nikkei.com/Life-Arts/Life/ Taiwan-s-enduring-fascination-with-Japanese-architecture.

Hille, Kathrin. "'I am Taiwanese': Czech Senate President Addresses Parliament in Taipei." *Financial Times,* September 1, 2020. https:// www.ft.com/content/fb018ddd-2591-4355-94b1-602ff2b025af.

Hioe, Brian. "Indigenous Occupation Calling for Return of Traditional Territories Reaches 1,000th Day." *New Bloom Magazine*, November 20, 2019. https://newbloommag.net/2019/11/20/indigenous-occupy-1000-days/.

———. "Indigenous Occupation in 228 Memorial Park Dismantled." *New Bloom Magazine*, March 14, 2022. https://newbloommag.net/2022/03 /14/indigenous-occupation-dismantled/.

Hsiao, Sherry. "Groups urge law to protect migrant domestic workers." *Taipei Times*, May 3, 2021, p. 3. https://www.taipeitimes.com/News/ taiwan/archives/2021/05/03/2003756749.

Hsu, Tiffany, Amy Chang Chien, and Steven Lee Myers. "Can Taiwan Continue to fight off Chinese Disinformation?" *New York Times*, November 26, 2023. https://www.nytimes.com/2023/11/26/business/media/taiwan-china-disinformation.html.

Huang, Joyce. "A Walk on the Mild Side." *Taiwan Review*, May 1, 2012. https://taiwantoday.tw/news.php?post=23680&unit=12,29,29,33,45.

"Jiefangjun zai Tai dao dongbu she ba bi tui 'ligen'hao" 解放军在台岛东部设靶逼退'里根'号 [The PLA targets pushing back the Reagan from eastern Taiwan]. *People's Daily*, August 5, 2022. http://tw.people.com.cn/n1/2022/0805/c14657-32495559.html.

Kao, Chia-ho, and Liu Tzu-hsuan, "Taiwan to have world's lowest birthrate by 2035." *Taipei Times*, November 2, 2022, p. 1. https://www.taipeitimes.com/News/front/archives/2022/11/02/2003788112.

Ko, Shu-ling, and Charles Snyder, "Chen says the NUC will 'cease'," *Taipei Times*, February 28, 2006, p. 1. https://www.taipeitimes.com/News/front/archives/2006/02/28/2003294988.

Kuo, Lily, and Alicia Chen. "Once a Covid success story, Taiwan struggles with a vaccine shortage." *Washington Post*, May 18, 2021, https://www.washingtonpost.com/world/asia_pacific/taiwan-virus-outbreak-covid-vaccines/2021/05/18/bba4c770-b6fa-11eb-bc4a-62849cf6cca9_story.html.

———. "Taiwan offered hope after they fled Hong Kong. Now, they're leaving again." *Washington Post*, May 31, 2022. https://www.washingtonpost.com/world/2022/05/31/taiwan-hong-kong-immigration-china/.

Kuo, Patricia. "Former fugitive designs monument." *Bowling Green Daily News* (Associated Press), February 20, 1994, p. 15c.

Lee, I-chia. "Chen and team rock Tainan on visit." *Taipei Times*, June 1, 2020. https://www.taipeitimes.com/News/front/archives/2020/06/01/2003737394.

Lee, Yi-an 李易安. "Bianjing shang de yixiangren" 邊境上的異鄉人 [The marginalized people of the borderlands]. *Duan chuanmei* 端傳媒 [The

Initium], January 4, 2021. https://theinitium.com/article/20210104-taiwan-km-generation-identity/.

Lin, Chia-nan. "False information on the rise in Taiwan: academic." *Taipei Times*, September 28, 2019, p. 3. https://www.taipeitimes.com/News/taiwan/archives/2019/09/28/2003723046.

Lin, Rebecca, Yi-shan Chen, Shu-ren Koo. "Han Kuo-yu's Visit to Hong Kong Raises Suspicions." *Tianxia zazhi* 天下雜誌 [*Commonwealth Magazine*], April 11, 2019. https://english.cw.com.tw/article/article.action?id=2354.

Liu, Fu-chuan 劉福全. "Shuangshi dadian dengchang You Si-kun: minzhu shi taiwan bainian jiyin ye yin minzhu cheng guoji buke huo que yi fenzi" 雙十大典登場 游錫堃：民主是台灣百年基因 也因民主成國際不可或缺一份子 [Double ten day ceremony speaker You Si-kun: Democracy has been in Taiwan's genes for 100 years, because of democracy it became an indispensable part of the world]. *Newtalk xinwen* 新聞 [*Newtalk News*], October 10, 2021. https://newtalk.tw/news/view/2021-10-10/649040.

Liu, Tzu-hsuan. "Taitung councilors oppose recognition of the Siraya." *Taipei Times*, June 29, 2022. https://www.taipeitimes.com/News/taiwan/archives/2022/06/29/2003780787.

Montlake, Simon. "The New Taiwanese." *The Wall Street Journal*, April 8, 2010.

"'New Constitution' means timetable for independence." *Zhongguo ribao* 中國日報 [*China Daily*]. April 14, 2005. http://www.chinadaily.com.cn/english/doc/2004-04/15/content_323377.htm.

Pan, Jason. "Miaoli migrant worker lockdown 'discriminatory.'" *Taipei Times*, July 29, 2022, p. 2. https://www.taipeitimes.com/News/taiwan/archives/2022/07/29/2003782618.

"President unveils four policies to help young people." *Focus Taiwan (CNA English News)*. December 5, 2019. https://www7.focustaiwan.tw/politics/201912050005.

Rauhala, Emily. "'Reunification Is a Decision to Be Made By the People Here:' Breakfast with Taiwan's Tsai Ing-wen." *Time Magazine*, June

18, 2015. https://time.com/magazine/south-pacific/3926185/june-29 th-2015-vol-185-no-24-asia-south-pacific/.

Robinson, Paul, and Emilia Terzon. "Taiwan flag design painted over by council ahead of beef industry event." *ABC News*, May 8, 2018. https://www.abc.net.au/news/2018-05-09/childrens-cow-statue-design-altered-taiwan-flag-painted-over-qld/9739574.

Shih, Gerry. "On China's Front Line, Emerging Cold War Haunts Battle-Worn Taiwanese Islands." *Washington Post*, September 10, 2020. https://www.washingtonpost.com/world/asia_pacific/china-taiwan-us-military-cold-war-kinmen/2020/09/09/c2a5caa6-e6bc-11ea-bf44-0 d31c85838a5_story.html.

Smith, Nicola. "Taiwanese official reveals China suspected 'human to human' transmission by January 13." *The Telegraph*, May 6, 2020. https://www.telegraph.co.uk/news/2020/05/06/taiwanese-official-reveals-china-suspected-human-human-transmission/.

Stone Fish, Isaac. "Stop Calling Taiwan a 'Renegade Province.'" *Foreign Policy*, January 15, 2016. https://foreignpolicy.com/2016/01/15/stop-calling-taiwan-a-renegade-province/.

Sun, Ta-chuan. "Indigenous Voices: The Cry of Taiwan's Aboriginal Peoples." *Taiwan Panorama*, March 2003. https://www.taiwan-panorama.com/en/Articles/Details?Guid=74f39b62-6547-48 b9-bdd2-3f3ef952379b&CatId=10&postname=Who%20Are%20the%2 0Aboriginal%20Peoples?.

"Taiwan's Bird Conservation Group Expelled from BirdLife International." *The News Lens International Edition*, September 16, 2020. https://international.thenewslens.com/article/140668.

"Taiwan Election Live Results." *Bloomberg News*, January 13, 2024. https://www.bloomberg.com/graphics/2024-taiwan-election/.

"Taiwan history museum to open in Tainan City." *Taiwan Today*, October 25, 2011. https://taiwantoday.tw/news.php?unit=10&post=18658.

"Taiwan protests MWC's labelling of Taiwan as Part of China." *Focus Taiwan (CNA English News)*, February 23, 2019, https://focustaiwan.tw/politics/201902230020.

"Tsai seeks to finalize conscription plan." *Taipei Times*, December 23, 2022, p. 1. https://www.taipeitimes.com/News/front/archives/2022/12/23/2003791231.

"US to donate 750,000 Covid vaccines to Taiwan: visiting senator." *Focus Taiwan (CNA English News)*, June 6, 2021. https://focustaiwan.tw/politics/202106060002.

Wang, Ann, and I-Hwa Cheng. "Taiwan Residents Largely Calm in the Face of Chinese Anger." *Reuters*, August 10, 2022. https://www.reuters.com/world/asia-pacific/taiwan-residents-largely-calm-face-chinese-anger-2022-08-10/.

Wang, Hsu-ching 王淑卿. "NHKの女性ベテランアナ ˋ台湾代表チームの名称正す" [NHK female veteran announcer corrects name of Taiwan's national team]. Zhongyang guangbo diantai 中央廣播電台 [Radio Taiwan International], July 25, 2021.

Wang, Joyu. "Taiwan's Defenses Against Information Warfare Gain Attention." *Wall Street Journal*, August 25, 2022. https://www.wsj.com/articles/taiwans-defenses-against-information-warfare-gain-attention-11661419802.

Wei, Clarissa. "The Topsy-Turvy End of Zero Covid in Taiwan." *New Yorker*, May 23, 2022. https://www.newyorker.com/news/dispatch/the-topsy-turvy-end-of-zero-covid-in-taiwan.

Wong, Chun Han. "China's Latest Taiwan Tactic Closes the Door on Individual Holidays to the Island." *Wall Street Journal*, July 31, 2019. https://www.wsj.com/articles/china-halts-individual-tours-to-taiwan-11564585028.

Wu Cheng-feng 吳政峰, "Xilayazu shi xian an xianfa fating shou bianlun" 西拉雅族釋憲案 憲法法庭首辯論 [First argument at court of the Siraya constitutional interpretation case], *Ziyou shibao*自由時報 [*Liberty Times*], June 29, 2022.

Wu, Po-wei, Chiu Yen-ling, and Jake Chung. "Aboriginal Land Boundary Draft Rules Meet Criticism." *Taipei Times*, February 16, 2017, p. 3. https://taipeitimes.com/News/taiwan/archives/2017/02/16/2003665090.

Xie, Tina. "A 24-hour Bookstore Turns its Final Page." *Taiwan Panorama* (*Taiwan guanghua zazhi* 台灣光華雜誌), May 2020. https://www. taiwanpanorama.com/Articles/Details?Guid=832d302b-bf5b-4757-8 b66-499b3b32e548&langId=3&CatId=8.

———. "Taroko Gorge from Multiple Angles." *Taiwan Panorama*, December 2021. https://www.taiwan-panorama.com/en/Articles/ Details?Guid=ac663ad4-af6b-47f5-a047-9ca3fad963d1&CatId=10.

Yang Bi-chuan 楊碧川. Trans. Aaron Wytze Wilson. "The 228 Massacre in Taipei: 'Forced Into a Car, Never to Return.'" *The Reporter*, February 20, 2017. https://www.twreporter.org/a/photos-228-taipei-english.

Yeh Su-ping 葉素萍. "Jinian wenxie bainian Cai zongtong pan wei shijie de taiwan jixu

tuanjie nuli" 紀念文協百年 蔡總統盼為世界的台灣繼續團結努力 [Commemorating the centennial of the Cultural Association: President Tsai hopes to unite and work hard for the world's Taiwan]. Zhongyang tongxunshe 中央通訊社 [Central News Agency], October 17, 2021. https://www.cna.com.tw/news/firstnews/202110170175. aspx.

Commentary, Analysis, and Editorials

Alton, Tom. "Taiwan's Covid-19 Response & 'Mask Diplomacy.'" *University of Alberta China Institute*, June 1, 2020. https://www. ualberta.ca/china-institute/media-library/media-gallery/research/ analysis-briefs/taiwan_mask_diplomacy.pdf.

Batto, Nathan. "The NPP's internal divisions, Ko's new party, and the China Cleavage." Frozen Garlic (blog), August 7, 2019. https:// frozengarlic.wordpress.com/2019/08/07/the-npps-internal-divisions- kos-new-party-and-the-china-cleavage/.

Beinart, Peter. "America needs an entirely new foreign policy for the Trump Age." *The Atlantic*, September 16, 2018. https:// www.theatlantic.com/ideas/archive/2018/09/shield-of-the-republic- a-democratic-foreign-policy-for-the-trump-age/570010/.

Bryan, Ed. "Taiwan: How Airlines Are Being Dragged into China's Bitter Dispute over the Island's Sovereignty." *The Conversation*, August

6, 2018. https://theconversation.com/taiwan-how-airlines-are-being-dragged-into-chinas-bitter-dispute-over-the-islands-sovereignty-100932.

Cheng, Cheng. "Taiwan's Unexpectedly Crazy Dating App Scene," *Tricky Taipei*, May 23, 2021. https://www.trickytaipei.com/taiwan-dating-apps/.

Chou, Catherine. "Island Utopia." *Inkstick Media*, April 29, 2020. https://inkstickmedia.com/island-utopia/.

———, and Gina Anne Tam. "Against 'One Country, Several Systems': Towards a New History of Taiwan and Hong Kong." *Radical History Review*, June 4, 2020. https://www.radicalhistoryreview.org/abusablepast/against-one-country-several-systems-towards-a-new-history-of-taiwan-and-hong-kong/.

Drun, Jessica. "Taiwan's Opposition Struggles to Shake Pro-China Image." *Foreign Policy*, March 11, 2020. https://foreignpolicy.com/2020/03/11/taiwan-opposition-kuomintang-kmt-pro-china-1992-consensus/.

———. "One China, Multiple Interpretations." Center for Advanced China Research, December 28, 2017. https://www.ccpwatch.org/single-post/2017/12/29/one-china-multiple-interpretations.

"Editorial: 'Bentu' Education Cannot Wait." *Taipei Times*, January 20, 2021, p. 8. https://www.taipeitimes.com/News/editorials/archives/2021/01/20/2003750875.

Fahey, Michael. "What Taiwan's Intermediate Skilled Manpower Classification Means." *The News Lens International*, September 27, 2022. https://international.thenewslens.com/article/173934.

Fang, Benson Ko-chou. "'Siren tudi gan ma yao yuanzhumin tongyi?' huan wo tudi zhengyi wangyou gezhong bu dong, daoli yuanlai shi zhe yang"「私人土地幹嘛要原住民同意？」還我土地爭議網友各種不懂，道理原來時這樣 ["'Why do indigenous Taiwanese have to agree to [use of] private land? What netizens don't understand about land disputes, it turns out the reasoning is this]. *Mata Taiwan*, February 18, 2017. https://www.matataiwan.com/2017/02/18/indigenous-people-land-right/.

Haggerty, Nicholas. "The Troublemaker: Chen Shui-bian Reconsidered, Part 1," *A Broad and Ample Road*, February 13, 2022. https://ampleroad.substack.com/p/the-troublemaker-chen-shui-bian-reconsidered.

Harrison, Mark. "Covid-19 Remapping East Asian Modernity." *Thesis Eleven*, August 12, 2020. https://thesiseleven.com/2020/08/12/covid-19-remapping-east-asian-modernity/.

Hioe, Brian. "The Dried Mango Strips of National Doom," *Popula*, November 6, 2019. https://popula.com/2019/11/06/the-dried-mango-strips-of-national-doom/.

———. "Between Infodemic and Pandemic: The Paranoid Style in Taiwanese Politics." *Popula*, July 22, 2021. https://popula.com/2021/07/22/between-infodemic-and-pandemic-the-paranoid-style-in-taiwanese-politics/.

Lai, You-hao. "Reform or Overreach? Constitutional Controversies in Taiwan's Recent Legislative Changes", *Taiwan Insight, Special Issue: Bluebird Movement: Legislative Reform Protests in Taiwan*, June 10, 2024. https://taiwaninsight.org/2024/06/10/reform-or-overreach-constitutional-controversies-in-taiwans-recent-legislative-changes/.

Lin, Cheng-yi. "Dodging the Covid Bullet: How Vaccine Donations by the US, Japan, and Lithuania Saved a Vulnerable Taiwan." *Prospects and Perspectives* 33 (published by Yuanjing jijinhui 遠景基金會 [Prospect Foundation]), July 7, 2021. https://www.pf.org.tw/en/pfen/33-8022.html.

Lin, Syaru Shirley. "It's not just China: Population, Power Generation, Political Polarization, and Parochialism are also Long-term Threats to Taiwan's Success and Survival," *China Leadership Monitor*, June 1, 2021. https://www.prcleader.org/lin-1.

Millward, James A. "We need a new approach to teaching modern Chinese history," *Medium.com* (blog), October 8, 2020, https://jimmillward.medium.com/we-need-a-new-approach-to-teaching-modern-chinese-history-we-have-lazily-repeated-false-d24983bd7ef2.

Morris, James X. "A Visual Dialogue of the 2014 Sunflower Movement, 5 Years Later." *The Diplomat*, April 26, 2019. https://thediplomat.

com/2019/04/a-visual-dialogue-of-the-2014-sunflower-movement-5-years-later/.

Rich, Timothy. "Does it matter if Taiwan loses formal recognition?" *East Asia Forum*, October 9, 2019. https://www.eastasiaforum.org/2019/10/09/does-it-matter-if-taiwan-loses-formal-recognition/.

Rowen, Ian. "Inside Taiwan's Sunflower Movement – Where Asia's Largest Student Uprising is Blooming." *Occupy.com*, April 4, 2014. https://www.occupy.com/article/inside-taiwans-sunflower-movement-%E2%80%93-where-asias-largest-student-uprising-blooming#sthash.aD4ln3qP.dpbs.

Rudd, Kevin. "How to Avoid a Crisis over Taiwan," *The Saturday Paper*, August 20, 2022. https://www.thesaturdaypaper.com.au/opinion/topic/2022/08/20/how-avoid-crisis-over-taiwan.

Sang, Huynh Tam. "Addressing Challenges Faced by Taiwan's Migrant Workers," *The Diplomat*, December 30, 2021. https://thediplomat.com/2021/12/addressing-challenges-faced-by-taiwans-migrant-workers/.

Stenberg, Josh. "'I am a Taiwanese': Eastern Europeans See a Cold War in East Asia." *The Interpreter*, August 5, 2021. https://www.lowyinstitute.org/the-interpreter/i-am-taiwanese-eastern-europeans-see-cold-war-east-asia.

Tan, Genevieve. "How Taiwan is using same-sex marriage to assert its national identity." *Washington Post*, June 26, 2019. https://www.washingtonpost.com/outlook/2019/06/26/how-taiwan-is-using-same-sex-marriage-assert-its-national-identity/.

"Target: Taiwan; America and China." *The Economist*, August 13, 2022, p. 9.

Tillett, Andrew. "China plans re-education once 'Taiwan is unified.'" *Australian Financial Review*, August 10, 2022. https://www.afr.com/politics/federal/no-room-for-compromise-over-taiwan-china-envoy-20220810-p5b8pz.

Turton, Michael. "Notes from Central Taiwan: A transition without justice," *Taipei Times*, September 13, 2021, p. 8. https://www.taipeitimes.com/News/feat/archives/2021/09/13/2003764273.

Wu, Albert. "The Black Iron Cage: Taiwanese Protesters in an Age of Global Unrest." *Los Angeles Review of Books*, June 3, 2014. https://lareviewofbooks.org/article/the-black-iron-cage-taiwanese-protesters-age-global-unrest/.

Xu Gongren, "Bierang muyu xiaoshi de jiyi" 別讓母語消失的記憶 [Don't let Your Mother Tongue be Lost to Memory] Zhonggushibao 中國時報 [China Times], November 8, 1997, 11.

Zhu, Zhiqun. "Why Taiwan is taking a hardline against unification with China – and what that means for the US." *Washington Post*, January 16, 2019. https://www.washingtonpost.com/outlook/2019/01/16/why-taiwan-is-taking-hard-line-against-unification-with-china-what-it-means-us/.

Multimedia

"Nimen zenme bu fennu! Yebaihe xueyun" 你們怎麼不憤怒！野百合學運) [Why aren't you angry? The Wild Lily Student Movement]. *Gongshi zhuti zhi ye* 公視主題之夜 [The subject this night]. Taiwan Public Television Station. May 12, 2016. YouTube video. https://www.youtube.com/watch?v=cCEnezIZbFA.

Tsai, Ching-ku 蔡靜菇, dir. *Women de 1990* 我們的1990 [Our 1990]. 2014; Taipei, Taiwan: Taipei Documentary Filmmakers Union. YouTube video. https://www.youtube.com/watch?v=6E-ZSfUO_AQ.

Think Tank Reports

Dickey, Lauren. "Confronting the Challenge of Online Disinformation in Taiwan," *Taiwan Security Brief: Disinformation, Cybersecurity, and Energy Challenges*, eds. Yuki Tatsumi, Pamela Kennedy, and Jason Li. Washington, DC: Stimson Center, 2019), 11–22. https://www.stimson.org/wp-content/files/file-attachments/StimsonTaiwanSecurityBrief2019.pdf.

Drun, Jessica, and Bonnie S. Glaser. The Distortion of UN Resolution 2758 and Limits on Taiwan's Access to the United Nations. Washington, DC: The German Marshall Fund, 2022. https://www.gmfus.org/news/

distortion-un-resolution-2758-and-limits-taiwans-access-united-nations.

Swaine, Michael, Jessica J. Lee, and Rachel Esplin Odell. "A New Direction: A Foreign Policy Playbook on Military Restraint for the Biden Team." Washington, DC: Quincy Institute for Responsible Statecraft, December 3, 2020. https://quincyinst.wpengine.com/wp-content/uploads/2020/12/A-New-Direction-Restraint-Playbook.pdf.

V-Dem Annual Report Team, "Democracy Facing Global Challenges: V-Dem Annual Democracy Report, 2019", Varieties of Democracy Institute, University of Gothenburg, May 2019, p. 34. https://v-dem.net/documents/16/dr_2019_CoXPbb1.pdf.

INDEX

ABOUT THE AUTHORS

Catherine Lila Chou is Assistant Professor of History at National Chengchi University in Taipei, Taiwan. For six years prior, she taught at Grinnell College in Iowa, where she was promoted to Associate Professor in 2024. She holds a PhD in early modern European history from Stanford University. Dr. Chou's work has appeared in *Historical Research, Parliamentary History, Journal of British Studies*, and *Historical Journal*.

Mark Harrison is Senior Lecturer in Chinese Studies at the University of Tasmania, Australia. He holds a PhD in Chinese Studies from Monash University in Melbourne, Australia. He is co-editor of the Brill Taiwan Studies Series and an Expert Associate of the National Security College of the Australian National University. His work on Taiwan has appeared in the *International Journal of Taiwan Studies, Thesis Eleven*, and in edited volumes such as *Re-writing Culture in Taiwan*.

CAMBRIA SINOPHONE WORLD SERIES

BOOKS IN THE CAMBRIA SINOPHONE WORLD SERIES

Revolutionary Taiwan: Making Nationhood in a Changing World Order by Catherine Lila Chou and Mark Harrison

Salvaging Buddhism to Save Confucianism in Choson Korea (1392–1910) by Gregory N. Evon

Sinophone Utopias: Exploring Futures Beyond the China Dream edited by Andrea Riemenschnitter, Jessica Imbach, and Justyna Jaguscik

Memory Making in Folk Epics of China: The Intimate and the Local in Chinese Regional Culture by Anne E. McLaren

Chinese Poetry as Soul Summoning: Shamanistic Religious Influences on Chinese Literary Tradition by Nicholas Morrow Williams

Taking China to the World: The Cultural Production of Modernity by Theodore Huters

Sensing the Sinophone: Urban Memoryscapes in Contemporary Fiction by Astrid Møller-Olsen

The Legend of Prince Golden Calf in China and Korea by Wilt L. Idema and Allard M. Olof

Individual Autonomy and Responsibility in Late Imperial China by Paolo Santangelo

Staging for the Emperors: A History of Qing Court Theatre, 1683–1923 by Liana Chen

Rethinking the Modern Chinese Canon: Refractions across the Transpacific by Clara Iwasaki

Decadence in Modern Chinese Literature and Culture: A Comparative and Literary-Historical Reevaluation by Hongjian Wang

Writing Poetry, Surviving War: The Works of Refugee Scholar-Official Chen Yuyi (1090–1139) by Yugen Wang

Monstrosity and Chinese Cultural Identity: Xenophobia and the Reimagination of Foreignness in Vernacular Literature since the Song Dynasty by Isaac Yue

Shaping Chinese Art History: Pang Yuanji and His Painting Collection by Katharine P. Burnett

Remapping the Contested Sinosphere: The Cross-cultural Landscape and Ethnoscape of Taiwan by Chia-rong Wu

Locating Taiwan Cinema in the Twenty-First Century edited by Paul G. Pickowicz and Yingjin Zhang

The Great Leap Backward: Forgetting and Representing the Mao Years by Lingchei Letty Chen

Rethinking the Sinosphere: Poetics, Aesthetics, and Identity Formation edited by Nanxiu Qian, Richard J. Smith, and Bowei Zhang

Reexamining the Sinosphere: Transmissions and Transformations in East Asia edited by Nanxiu Qian, Richard J. Smith, and Bowei Zhang

Insects in Chinese Literature: A Study and Anthology by Wilt L. Idema

The Poetics and Politics of Sensuality in China: The "Fragrant and Bedazzling" Movement (1600–1930) by Xiaorong Li

Spatial Imaginaries in Mid-Tang China: Geography, Cartography, and Literature by Ao Wang

Texts and Transformations: Essays in Honor of the 75th Birthday of Victor H. Mair edited by Haun Saussy

Chinese Women Writers and Modern Print Culture by Megan M. Ferry

Reading Lu Xun Through Carl Jung by Carolyn Brown

Gao Xingjian and Transmedia Aesthetics edited by Mabel Lee and Liu Jianmei

Imperfect Understanding: Intimate Portraits of Chinese Celebrities edited by Christopher Rea

Zhang Yimou: Globalization and the Subject of Culture by Wendy Larson

The Borderlands of Asia: Culture, Place, Poetry by Mark Bender

Buddhist Transformations and Interactions: Essays in Honor of Antonino Forte edited by Victor H. Mair

Chinese Avant-garde Fiction: Quest for Historicity and Transcendent Truth by Zhansui Yu

Eroticism and Other Literary Conventions in Chinese Literature: Intertextuality In The Story Of The Stone by I-Hsien Wu

The Sinophone Cinema of Hou Hsiao-hsien: Culture, Style, Voice and Motion by Christopher Lupke

Supernatural Sinophone Taiwan and Beyond by Chia-rong Wu

Cosmopolitanism in China edited by Minghui Hu and Johan Elverskog

"The Immortal Maiden Equal to Heaven" and Other Precious Scrolls from Western Gansu by Wilt L. Idema

Chinese Ethnic Minority Oral Traditions: A Recovered Text of Bai Folk Songs in a Sinoxenic Script by Jingqi Fu and Zhao Min with Xu Lin and Duan Ling

China and Beyond in the Mediaeval Period: Cultural Crossings and Inter-Regional Connections edited by Dorothy C. Wong and Gustav Heldt

Anglophone Literatures in the Asian Diaspora: Literary Transnationalism and Translingual Migrations by Karen An-hwei Lee

Modern Poetry in China: A Visual-Verbal Dynamic by Paul Manfredi

Sinophone Malaysian Literature: Not Made in China by Alison M. Groppe

Infected Korean Language, Purity versus Hybridity: From the Sinographic Cosmopolis to Japanese Colonialism to Global English by Koh Jongsok (translated by Ross King)

The Chinese Prose Poem: A Study of Lu Xun's Wild Grass (Yecao) by Nicholas A. Kaldis

Gao Xingjian: Aesthetics and Creation by Gao Xingjian (translated by Mabel Lee)

Rethinking Chineseness: Translational Sinophone Identities in the Nanyang Literary World by E. K. Tan

A Study of Two Classics: A Cultural Critique of The Romance of the Three Kingdoms and The Water Margin by Liu Zaifu (translated by Shu Yunzhong)

Confucian Prophet: Political Thought in Du Fu's Poetry (752–757) by David K. Schneider

The Classic of Changes in Cultural Context: A Textual Archaeology of the "Yi jing" by Scott Davis

9 781638 571957